God is King!

God is King!

Tom Wells

 EVANGELICAL PRESS

EVANGELICAL PRESS
12 Wooler Street, Darlington, Co. Durham, DL1 1RQ, England

© Evangelical Press 1992
First published 1992

British Library Cataloguing in Publication Data available

ISBN 0 85234 297 7

Other books by Tom Wells:
A Vision for Missions
Come to Me
Faith: the Gift of God
The Moral Basis of Faith
Christian: Take Heart!
A Price for a People

Printed and bound in Great Britain by Bath Press, Avon.

Contents

Part I

Getting started

A few words of introduction

In an earlier book I wrote about the way people often react when I mention the sovereignty of God. Christians, I find, want immediately and emphatically to be counted among those who believe in God's kingship. 'I too believe in the sovereignty of God,' they say, as though to deny such a thing would invite fire from heaven. One cannot be too quick to confess that God is King: that seems to be the spirit in which they respond.

I guess that is all to the good, but still I have my doubts. Why? Because most Christians are more than a little uneasy in seeing God's kingship at work in their daily lives. Or at least that is the way it seems to me. Some speak of so-called 'natural disasters' as evidence that God is at work (especially when those 'disasters' come to others). Many, however, will not go that far. Unless something is clearly a 'blessing', a positive and enjoyable experience, they are not ready to say that it comes from God. In fact, they will often firmly deny it. 'God is love,' they say, or 'God is too good to have caused this to happen.' And in that way they eliminate God from much of the world he has made. They do not mean to do that, but that is what I think they do.

I also see Christians who look at life in another way. They seem willing enough to say that their own difficulties — disasters even — come from God, because 'God wants to teach me something.' Their approach, however, suggests that God's intervention in day-to-day life is an uncommon event with a special message. Life normally goes on without much contact with the sovereignty of God. Only denseness or disobedience on their part leads God to assert his authority, to exercise his kingship. When they have learned their lesson God steps aside until they need correcting again.

Finally, some Christians try to combine the two views I have outlined. Because the Scriptures so often show us God's kingship, many believers look at both blessing and difficulty as coming from his hand. But that creates its own problems. It raises questions about the extent of God's control in this world. Surely it is too simple to say that God does everything that is done, and leave it at that. But if we cannot say that, what can we say? Sooner or later, then, we must ask ourselves something like this: God is King, but what does that mean?

1.
The importance of our standpoint

Not long ago I heard of a woman who raised questions about God's part in our daily lives. I will put what she asked as bluntly as possible, so that you cannot miss its importance. 'If there really is a God, why does he treat me the way he does? My life seems to be one frustration after another! Where's the fairness in that?' I do not doubt that you have heard these same questions more than once; perhaps you have even asked them yourself.

These are not easy questions. Sometimes I have thought that I knew why this or that thing happened to me, but usually I have not. Now and then I have said that God was teaching me a certain lesson by what I went through, but most of the time I have been in the dark about the meaning of my trials. I have had my frustrations, and generally speaking I have not known why. Perhaps your experience has been different from mine; I do not know, but I do not think that I am unusual. Many times I could have asked, 'Why did that thing happen to me, and not something else?' I did not know then, and I do not know now.

Someone may ask, 'If you don't know the answers to these kinds of questions, why do you bring them up?' My reason is this: I am concerned about the standpoint from which we ask our questions. After all, do you and I have the right to ask God about the fairness of his dealings with us? Does the Lord owe us an explanation when he drops difficulties into our paths? Must he prove that he has acted fairly? We really must face these questions before we demand reasons from God.

Now please do not misunderstand me. I do not doubt that God

does what is just and fair with all his creatures. I do not question that, and I do not want you to question it. But it is one thing to believe that God is just, and it is something else to demand that he explain to me and to you the justice of what he is doing at the moment. If we were not so emotionally involved in what happens to us, we would be able to see the distinction between these two things.

But why would God not let you know in detail what he is doing? There are many reasons. For instance, what God is doing with you just now is intricately woven into his larger activity in all the earth. Is there time enough for you to grasp all his work in the world, so that you will understand what he is doing with you? Obviously not. Again, how many things is God doing with us today? Ten? 100? 1,000? Remember that every atom that touches us affects us in some way! Questions like these help us to see that the answer to 'why?' may be well beyond our understanding at the time we want an explanation. They ought to humble us, and help us to change our point of view on God's activity. They should certainly keep us from complaining against God.

But there is an even more serious point that needs to be made. The question, 'Why does God treat me the way he does?' often comes up because I have a wrong view of my life. I look on myself as an end in myself. But suppose I am a means, and not an end; what then? Please follow me closely here. I do not want us to get bogged down in the terms I am using — 'means' and 'ends' — terms that seem unrelated to our daily lives, but they are important. They stand for two very different ways of seeing myself and the God who made me. What does it mean to think of myself as an end? It means that God can have no designs or plans for me unless they fit in with my own plans and goals for my life. It means that he cannot use me in any way without asking what I want. If I am an end, then I exist for my own purposes and not for his. In answer to the question, 'Why does God treat me this way?', I can never be satisfied with an answer that centres on God. If I am an end, then I must reject the reply that says, 'Because it pleased him!'

But all this changes if I see myself as a means to God's ends. If I am a means, then the words 'because it pleased him' make a lot of sense. They remind me that God has a right to do with me as he pleases. They tell me again that I am not the Creator; he is. My thinking changes because I see myself in a different light. I have taken a new standpoint.

If you cannot bring yourself to think of yourself as a means to God's ends you will never get any help with the question, 'Why does God treat me as he does?' Your false standpoint will defeat you right from the start. Think about those two words again: means and end! Which are you? Much of your future happiness is likely to depend on how you answer that question. It is not a case of my trying to force you into submission on this matter. Not at all! It is simply a question of reality. Paul put it this way: 'For from [God] and through him and to him are all things' (Rom.11:36). The words 'to him' tell why God made you. You do not exist for your own ends. You exist for your Creator's ends. That is the teaching of Scripture.

We can approach this matter of standpoint in another way. Here are the words of the Lord Jesus: 'I tell you the truth, unless you change and become like little children, you will never enter the kingdom of heaven' (Matt. 18:3). We all know that a child sees things differently from an adult. That is the point of Jesus' remark. In some ways, of course, we must grow beyond spiritual childhood and become mature men and women, but in other ways we must remain children. Should we ever outgrow simple trust in our heavenly Father? Surely not!

God has not left Christians to think of him merely as their Creator. It is important to know that we are his creatures, but every believer is also a child of God. If we remember that fact we will do what a child must constantly do: we will trust our Father where we cannot understand. In my book, *Faith: the Gift of God,* I put it this way: 'So, what can I do? I'll tell you what I have done, and what I think you must do. I have fallen back on the character of God.

'*God is just.* That means that he will never plan an injustice — not to any man, not to the wickedest sinner who ever lived. *God is also wise.* That means that he knows how to carry out his just plans. There is no question of his not knowing what injustice is. *God is all-powerful too.* He never lacks the resources to put his justice into effect. The answer to our difficulties, you see, lies in the character of God.

'And *God has designed things that way.* That is the reason we know no more than we do. It is not our lack of spirituality or our denseness when compared to other Christians. In fact, the more "spiritual" Christians — whoever they may be — have the same intellectual problems that we have. God has made things that way.

And, of course, he made them that way because he wanted to. And there we must leave the problem.'[1]

In that quotation I have described the attitude of a child. The subject matter is way over the head of a youngster, but the point of view is the same. Where does a child leave his intellectual problems (even though he knows nothing of the word 'intellectual')? He leaves them with his parents, and he trusts them.

Let me illustrate this further. Think of yourself as a child about to enrol in school for the first time. What course will you take? Well, that is all settled for you. If you were an adult you might look over a catalogue or brochure that contains many choices, but you are only a child and unable to choose wisely for yourself. The course, at first, is the same as the programme for all your fellow students. That is the way it is when you start out; and that is the way it is with a Christian. You have to learn the basics, the fundamentals. You start with faith. You are a creature, ready to learn about your Creator, but more than that, if you have come to Christ, you are a child that must trust his Father. The course is a long one, and seldom easy. One important lesson is the subject of this book: God is King, but what does that mean?

Reference
1. T. Wells, *Faith: the Gift of God*, Banner of Truth Trust, 1983, pp.147-8.

Part II

God's kingship over circumstances and events

2.
Introducing God's kingship

God is King, but what is a king? There are two ways to answer that question. The first way is to give a definition. I will try to do that in a moment. The second way is to show a king in action. Since each king has his own style, we will look at the actions of God himself. All other kings are pale imitations of the Lord of heaven and earth.

In simplest terms a king is a *ruler*. Synonyms of king include 'sovereign', 'monarch', 'potentate', 'emperor' and 'tzar'. But the basic idea remains the same in all of these words: the idea of a ruler. If God is King — and he is — then God is Ruler.

The word 'ruler' carries with it two ideas. The first is the idea of *authority*. A ruler ought to have authority, or the right to rule. The second idea is *the exercise of authority*. We do not think of a person as a ruler if he never rules anything. Normally a ruler exercises his right to rule. If he does not do so, he is not a ruler in the common usage of the word.

Now let us see how these two ideas apply to God. Does God have the authority, the right, to rule this world? Yes, he does. He has that right because he made the world. The heavens and the earth belonged to him when he made them. He could do with them as he pleased. And nothing has changed; they are still his. David wrote, 'The earth is the Lord's, and everything in it, the world, and all who live in it' (Ps. 24:1). Why does it belong to the Lord? Because he is its Creator. 'For he founded it upon the seas and established it upon the waters' (Ps. 24:2). Creation and ownership go together. No wonder Moses told Israel, 'To the Lord your God belong the heavens, even the highest heavens, the earth and everything in it' (Deut. 10:14).

God himself asserts his ownership:

'I have no need of a bull from your stall
    or of goats from your pens,
for every animal of the forest is mine,
    and the cattle on a thousand hills.
I know every bird in the mountains,
    and the creatures of the field are mine.
If I were hungry I would not tell you,
    for the world is mine, and all that is in it'

(Ps. 50:9-12).

I have said that creation and ownership go together. That is part of what God is saying here, but he also makes something else clear. He has the right to rule his creation, even to the point of using up the animals for food or for sacrifice. No authority to rule can reach further than the power to destroy life.

David ties together ownership and the right to rule in his prayer (and notice especially the places where I add italics):

'Praise be to you, O Lord,
    God of our father Israel,
    from everlasting to everlasting.
Yours, O Lord, is the greatness and the power
    and the glory and the majesty and the splendour,
    for everything in heaven and earth is yours.
Yours, O Lord, is the kingdom;
    you are exalted as head over all.
Wealth and honour come from you;
    you are the ruler of all things'

(1 Chron. 29:11-12).

'Everything in heaven and earth' belongs to God, and 'You are the ruler of all things.' The two go hand in hand. We may not question God's authority, his right to rule.

But how far does God exercise his right to rule? That is what we really want to know. That is what the people I talk to are concerned about. Nothing is easier than to get Christians to agree that God has the right, the authority, to rule the world he has made, but how far he actually exercises that authority is the point of contention. Yet the

Bible speaks clearly on that point, and we need to find out what it says.

In this section of the book I want us to look at God's kingship over our circumstances and events. It seems to me that there are three ways to approach this subject from the Scriptures. These three ways will form the outline of what I say in this and the following chapters of this section.

1. God's kingship is seen in direct statements about it in Scripture.
2. God's kingship is revealed incidentally by what Scripture tells us on other subjects.
3. God's kingship is suggested by reflection on what Scripture tells us about his nature.

Think with me of the moment when God created the heavens and the earth. At that moment all that existed conformed to the will of God. The circumstances of that day were what they were because the Lord made them that way. That was true on each succeeding day of creation. Before God created angels and men he was the only personal agent in the universe. His will was the only will in all creation. Looking back over his work God was able to pronounce it all 'very good' (Gen. 1:31). It was good because it was the way God wanted it to be.

Then something happened. We have few details of the fall of Satan and the army of spirits that joined him in his revolt against God. But his fall, and the later fall of man, brought about a new situation. Now there was a clash of wills in the world, God commanding one thing and men and fallen angels doing something else. Here, in other words, was rebellion against the rule of God. How did God react to this? Did he give up his rule? No, he did not.

What do we think when we hear of a clash of wills? We are likely to suppose that God has lost control, that he is no longer able to rule. But we must not think that at all. The circumstances around us and the events of our lives are as really in God's control as they were before man fell. There is a difference in the way God exercises his rule since men and angels revolted. We know that fallen beings do not freely follow God's commands as they once did. That much is clear. But we must not let that fact confuse us. God has more than one way of getting his plans carried out.

To explain what I mean let me quote from my earlier book, *A Vision for Missions:* 'Adam made a frontal attack on the sovereignty of God. In effect, Adam said: "You have been King till now. But now I shall be king. Now I will pursue my own purposes. Your lordship, God, is over." Fallen man sets himself up in competition to the God he sinned against. This is what sin does. It seeks to dethrone God. Sin snatches at his crown. Sin says: "Away with the sovereignty of God!"

'But we must slow down. We must not move too fast. The question is: Does sin succeed? Are God's purposes thwarted by sin? And the answer to that question is remarkable. It is not at all what we might have expected. The answer is this: Adam the sinner furthered the purposes of God to the same degree as Adam the righteous. He did not aim to do so, but that is what Adam did.

'Before I seek to prove this from Scripture, let us try to understand what it means. Please note what I did *not* say. I did not say that Adam furthered the purposes of God *in the same way* as Adam the righteous. Not at all! Adam the righteous sought to please God and to serve God as his Lord. Adam the sinner did the opposite. His way was wholly different. The new way was the reverse of the old — what is sometimes called "an 180° turn". No one could confuse Adam's new intention with his old one.

'But Adam's intention is not the whole story. What Adam aimed to do and what Adam actually managed to do are not the same. In a different way, but *in the same degree,* Adam carried forward the purpose of God. Adam's act was sinful because he did not aim to please God. His motive was wrong, and God judged him for it. But God meant to use even that evil to advance his own glory.

'To see this more clearly, let us compare it with the story of the sin of Joseph's brothers, given later in Genesis. Joseph's brothers hated him. For that reason Joseph was a marked young man. Time was on the brothers' side. Sooner or later their chance to dispose of him would come. And they would do it with relish.

'The day finally came. Midianite slave-traders passed near the spot where the brothers were tending their flocks, and his brothers sold Joseph into slavery. The deal netted them twenty pieces of silver, and they washed their hands of Joseph for ever. Or so they thought.

'In fact, their act proved to be only the beginning of the story. When famine later struck Canaan, the brothers were forced to go down into Egypt to buy grain. And what did they find? They found Joseph — not now a slave, but the virtual ruler of Egypt — and they were at his mercy.

'The story has a happy end, but only because Joseph understood the ways of God. Joseph saw more in the events of his life than the brothers' hatred. Later, when they pleaded for forgiveness, we read: "Joseph wept when they spoke unto him. And his brethren also went and fell down before his face; and they said, Behold, we be thy servants. And Joseph said unto them, Fear not: for am I in the place of God? But as for you, ye thought evil against me; but God meant it unto good, to bring to pass, as it is this day, to save much people alive" (Genesis 50:17-19).

'Now what has Joseph done here? He has laid his finger, has he not, on two sets of intentions, where his brothers saw but one? They intended to be done with him. And, of course, that was their sin — a sin for which they must answer. But Joseph sees more. He sees the aim of God. Israel had to find its way to Egypt, so God sent Joseph ahead to prepare a place for them. When the brothers sold Joseph they cared nothing for the purpose of God. Nevertheless, they brought it about. The sin was theirs, but the act was God's. In this, as in all else, God was King and they were his unwitting servants. The sovereignty of God held against the sinful aim of man. They, like Adam, defied God ... and they, like Adam, carried out his purpose!'[1]

Amazing though it may seem, wicked persons can be unwitting servants of God! That is, they may serve him and never know that they are doing so. Even if Satan creates the circumstances they will further God's plans.

Reference
1. T Wells, *A Vision for Missions,* Banner of Truth Trust, 1985, pp.44-7.

3.
God and Satan

Dozens of Scripture texts bear out the truth I illustrated in the last chapter. They tell us that God gets his will done in every place, at all times and through all persons. Not even Satan is an exception. If we find that Satan carries out God's purposes, it will not be hard to believe that others do so too.

Do you remember the story of Paul's thorn in the flesh? Paul was writing to the Corinthian church. He had just told them of a great vision God had given him, so great in fact that he was in danger of being puffed up about it. Then he goes on: 'To keep me from becoming conceited because of these surpassingly great revelations, there was given me a thorn in my flesh, a messenger of Satan, to torment me. Three times I pleaded with the Lord to take it away from me. But he said to me, "My grace is sufficient for you, for my power is made perfect in weakness"' (2 Cor. 12:7-9).

There are several points of interest here. The most obvious is that Paul did not bring about this circumstance in his life. We do not know what his thorn was, but whatever it was, it was put on him by someone else. Another person was king over Paul in this matter. Now the question is, who was it? Who created this circumstance? Who gave Paul his 'thorn in the flesh'? Read the passage again, if you like, and then try to answer the question.

Is the answer, Satan? Yes, but... Yes, Satan gave Paul his thorn, but there is a good deal more than Satan's work in this passage. I think I can bring it out by asking another question. Did Satan care if Paul swelled up with pride until he burst? Remember what Paul says. He tells us that he received his thorn to keep him from becoming conceited. No, Satan would have been pleased if Paul had become useless to God through pride.

What was going on, then? Here is what happened: Satan did his worst to Paul, but in doing it he was only able to further the purposes of God. No doubt Satan's aim was to torment Paul — and he succeeded! Why else would Paul have called this thing 'a thorn'? The thorn, whatever it was, brought Paul pain. That is why he prayed to have it removed. So, in a sense, Satan got his way with Paul. But this in no way thwarted God's plans for Paul and the spread of the gospel. In fact, Satan played into God's hands by what he did! He could do nothing else, because God is King.

That brings me to the other point that is vital here. I said that Satan was doing his worst to Paul. But what did I mean by that? We can think of things worse than a thorn in the flesh. Satan could have totally disabled Paul. Surely that would have been worse than what he did. Suppose he had killed Paul? That would have been far worse, wouldn't it? From the standpoint of the spread of the gospel, destroying Paul would have been a master stroke. Why not kill Paul, then?

I am sure you are way ahead of me here. When I said that Satan did his worst, I meant that Satan did the worst thing that God would let him do. Satan was not allowed to kill Paul, but he could give Paul a thorn, so that is what he did. He did what he could.

We see God's kingship over these circumstances in two ways. First, God made sure that his own purpose was carried out. His purpose was to keep Paul humble and useful. Second, he limited what Satan could do. These two things brought about the circumstance that Paul found himself in. God, you see, was King over whatever it was that happened to Paul, yet Satan was not a mere puppet in all this. He did what he wanted to do, within limits. You and I are not puppets even though we have to work within the boundaries that parents or employers put around us. In something of the same way Satan takes his own path, but he carries forward God's plans as he does it.

Indeed God's plans are so completely carried out that in a sense we may say that God is the one who does whatever happens in the world — *in a sense*. I repeat those last three words because, as we shall see, God is not the author of sin, and men are not puppets. In what sense God is the one who does all things may be difficult to grasp, but we shall see that the Bible sometimes speaks of him as doing the things that Satan and wicked men do. My next illustration will show what I mean.

Think about the story of Job. Satan was standing before God one day when God said, 'Have you considered my servant Job? There is no one on earth like him; he is blameless and upright, a man who fears God and shuns evil' (Job 1:8). That was high praise! But see what happened next: '"Does Job fear God for nothing?" Satan replied. "Have you not put a hedge around him and his household and everything he has? You have blessed the work of his hands, so that his flocks and herds are spread throughout the land. But stretch out your hand and strike everything he has, and he will surely curse you to your face." The Lord said to Satan, "Very well, then, everything he has is in your hands, but on the man himself do not lay a finger"' (Job 1:9-12).

This is much like Paul's experience. Here too Satan is going to torment one of God's people and, as in Paul's case, he will do it within the limits which God has set, and its goal will be to further God's purposes in Job's life. It will help Job, just as it helped Paul!

Satan wastes no time. In quick succession Job hears of heart-stabbing losses. The Sabeans steal his oxen and donkeys and kill their herdsmen. Fire from heaven destroys his sheep and their shepherds. Chaldean raiders drive his camels away and murder their keepers. But all of this is child's play compared to the final blow: 'Another messenger came and said, "Your sons and daughters were feasting and drinking wine at the oldest brother's house, when suddenly a mighty wind swept in from the desert and struck the four corners of the house. It collapsed on them and they are dead, and I am the only one who has escaped to tell you!"' (Job 1:18-19). If we have any feeling, we are not surprised that Job was soon wishing he had never been born.

There is, however, something even more important which we can learn if we look closely at his first reaction. Here it is: 'At this, Job got up and tore his robe and shaved his head. Then he fell to the ground in worship and said:

"Naked I came from my mother's womb,
    and naked I will depart.
The Lord gave and the Lord has taken away;
    may the name of the Lord be praised."'

'In all this, Job did not sin by charging God with wrongdoing' (1:20-22)

What do we see? First, worship! But what is the heart of that worship? Job says, 'The Lord gave *and the Lord has taken away;* may the name of the Lord be praised.' Note the words I have put in italics. Can we say that Job blamed the Lord for these calamities? No, there was no blame. This was an act of adoration. Job's view was this: God caused his losses. The Lord took back his former gifts. All was the Lord's work. God did it!

But suppose someone says, 'It's all well and good to cite these words of Job to show that God brought on his calamities, but Job cannot be held responsible for what he said at a time like that! How would you feel if that happened to you? What would you say?' Well, of course, I do not know what I would say. Something I would later be ashamed of, I suspect. But look at verse 22: 'In all this, Job did not sin by charging God with wrongdoing.' Here the author of Job has gone ahead of us. He has met the objection head-on. When Job said that God took away his goods, Job was right. That is the author's position. Job and the inspired writer agree: 'The Lord has taken away.' God did it.

In chapter 2 another crushing blow falls on Job. Satan attacks his body. Painful sores cover him from top to toe. Then his wife breaks under the burden of their tragedy. 'Curse God,' she says, 'and die!' Job's reply is significant: 'You are talking like a foolish woman. Shall we accept good from God, and not trouble?' In other words, 'God is doing this!' Has Job overstepped a creature's bounds in accusing the Lord? Here is the author's comment: 'In all this, Job did not sin in what he said' (Job 2:9-10). Again Job and the inspired writer agree: God did it! Job's trouble — trouble that we know came directly from Satan — was trouble from the hand of God. Does that seem too bold? Then look at this, from the end of the book: 'All [Job's] brothers and sisters ... consoled him *over all the trouble the Lord had brought upon him*' (Job 42:11). The trouble was the work of God.

Why does the writer of Scripture speak of Job's trouble as the work of the Lord? Because the plans that work out are God's plans, not Satan's. The Lord humbles Job. He teaches Job to know him more fully. He confronts Job with his greatness and glory. Finally the Lord brings Job to this remarkable confession:

'My ears had heard of you
    but now my eyes have seen you.
Therefore I despise myself
    and repent in dust and ashes'

(Job 42:6).

This is hardly the end that Satan had in view when he provoked the Lord against Job!

Let me illustrate what I mean with these two columns:

God's purpose	Satan's purpose
God aimed to lead Job to know God better than he knew him before.	Satan aimed to lead God to know Job better than he knew him before.

Which of them succeeded? The answer is obvious. God carried out his plan. Satan, on the other hand, failed to reach his goal of showing Job to be a parasite on God. No wonder that Job and the writer agree that the Lord did it. The chief workman in Job's distress was the living God!

One more story from the Old Testament will show the same thing. In 2 Samuel we read: 'Again the anger of the Lord burned against Israel, and he incited David against them, saying, "Go and take a census of Israel and Judah"' (2 Sam. 24:1). Who moved David to take a census? The Lord. But compare that fact with this statement in the account in 1 Chronicles: 'Satan rose up against Israel and incited David to take a census of Israel' (1 Chron. 21:1). Now who moved David? Satan. Here the writers of Scripture trace the same event back to both God and the devil. Is this a contradiction? If you do not see that Satan does the work of God *in some sense*, it is hard to explain these texts. But when you see that Satan serves God's purposes, though he does not mean to, then the texts become clear. Satan is the unwitting and unwilling servant of God. Joseph's brothers furthered God's plans by selling Joseph into Egypt. This was not their intention but that is what they did. It is the same with Satan. Satan forwards God's programme when he puts his wicked plans into action. That is not what he wants to do, but that is what he does.

We may see the same thing in the Lord Jesus' earthly life. Satan and Jesus were enemies — that much is plain. Yet Satan had a ministry to perform in the life of Jesus! Does that seem remarkable, impossible even? It is true. After Jesus' baptism we read, 'Then Jesus was led by the Spirit into the desert to be tempted by the devil' (Matt. 4:1). Why did the Spirit lead Jesus into the desert? Was it a pleasant place to spend a few days? Hardly! The Spirit of God had a far more serious purpose, and that purpose had to be carried out. Satan had to tempt Jesus, so that this could be said of him: 'For we do not have a high priest who is unable to sympathize with our weaknesses, but we have one who has been tempted in every way, just as we are — yet was without sin' (Heb. 4:15). Or again: 'Because he himself suffered when he was tempted, he is able to help those who are being tempted' (Heb. 2:18). God was King in the temptation of Jesus, as in all else. Satan served God's purposes.

Here is one more example. Paul had to rebuke the church at Corinth because they tolerated immorality. He writes, 'A man has his father's wife. And you are proud!' (1 Cor. 5:1-2). There is shock and anger in his words. How could the Corinthian believers put up with this? They needed to take steps immediately to get rid of this cancer. Now watch what Paul commanded them to do: 'When you are assembled in the name of our Lord Jesus and I am with you in spirit, and the power of our Lord Jesus is present, hand this man over to Satan, so that the sinful nature may be destroyed and his spirit saved on the day of the Lord' (1 Cor. 5:4-5). Paul told them to 'hand this man over to Satan'! His object was that the man might be saved at the day of the Lord!

I am not certain what 'handing over to Satan' meant to the church at Corinth. At the very least it meant expelling him from the fellowship — perhaps much more. But the Corinthians knew what Paul wanted, and that is the important thing. Whatever it was, Paul had it done so that the immoral man might be saved. Now ask yourself these questions: 'Would Satan co-operate in bringing a man to Christ? Would Satan help an erring believer towards repentance?' I would not have thought so, would you? But Paul did! Did Paul have confidence in Satan? To ask the question is to answer it. No, of course not! But Paul did trust God, and that meant that if this immoral man was one of God's elect, God would see to it that the way Satan handled him would help bring him to Christ. Satan, you see, would have to serve the purposes of God. Here also, God is King.

In the next chapter we will look at how wicked men also further

God's purposes. That too is an important fact. But before we turn to that subject let me remind you of something else. When we speak of the way the acts of ungodly men serve God's goals, we are not really leaving the subject of Satan. Many times he lies behind the deeds of men. The acts of sinners are often inspired by the devil. God, however, remains King through it all.

4.
God and wicked men

The Bible teaches that God controls wicked men. That does *not* mean that they do not sin. Far from it! They sin freely, and God is not the author of their sin. Their sin is their own. Despite that, all they do serves God's purposes. God is King, even over the ungodly. Does the Bible really teach this? Let us see.

A good place to start will be with political figures. Some think that the world of politics is especially corrupt. In Bible times the chief politicians were often kings. Was God King over these kings? Yes, he was.

First we learn that *God raises some to political power and removes others to make room for them.* Mary sang:

'[God] has performed mighty deeds with his arm ...
He has brought down rulers from their thrones
      but has lifted up the humble'

(Luke 1:51-52).

The Old Testament richly illustrates her words. Take as an example the Pharaoh who ruled Egypt in Moses' time. After God had sent seven plagues on Egypt he moved Moses to tell Pharaoh: 'For by now I could have stretched out my hand and struck you and your people with a plague that would have wiped you off the earth. But I have raised you up for this very purpose, that I might show you my power and that my name might be proclaimed in all the earth' (Exod. 9:15-16). Who raised Pharaoh to the throne of Egypt? God did. And in these verses he reminded Pharaoh that he could remove him from the earth whenever he wanted to.[1]

When Israel later rebelled against God's rule by wanting a king like other nations, God selected their king for them. Samuel the prophet was about to meet Saul, a man of Benjamin. The Scripture says, 'Now the day before Saul came, the Lord had revealed this to Samuel: "About this time tomorrow I will send you a man from the land of Benjamin. Anoint him leader over my people Israel..." When Samuel caught sight of Saul, the Lord said to him, "This is the man I spoke to you about; he will govern my people"' (1 Sam. 9:15-17).

Saul was a striking man, the kind of leader the people themselves might have chosen. But not long after, Saul showed he was not willing to follow the Lord, so God rejected him. When Samuel seemed reluctant to give up on Saul, we read, 'The Lord said to Samuel, "How long will you mourn for Saul, since I have rejected him as king over Israel? Fill your horn with oil and be on your way; I am sending you to Jesse of Bethlehem. I have chosen one of his sons to be king"' (1 Sam.16:1).

In this way David came on the scene of history. Mary's song might have been written with David in mind. He was a 'humble' man in many senses, the youngest of Jesse's sons. He did not seem impressive, but the Lord told Samuel, 'The Lord does not look at the things man looks at. Man looks at the outward appearance, but the Lord looks at the heart' (1 Sam. 16:7). None of the people would have taken David for a king at this time in his life. But God had chosen him, and he would see to it that David would rule.

Our next example is a dramatic one. Through the prophet Daniel, God told Nebuchadnezzar, King of Babylon: 'You will be driven away from people and will live with the wild animals; you will eat grass like cattle and be drenched with the dew of heaven ... until you acknowledge that the Most High is sovereign over the kingdoms of men and gives them to anyone he wishes' (Dan. 4:25).

Nebuchadnezzar supposed that his own power had made him king. He thought that his glory was life's highest end: 'Twelve months later, as the king was walking on the roof of the royal palace of Babylon, he said, "Is not this the great Babylon I have built as the royal residence, by my mighty power and for the glory of my majesty?"'

That was God's cue. The King of kings acted: 'The words were still on his lips when a voice came from heaven, "This is what is decreed for you, King Nebuchadnezzar: Your royal authority has been taken from you"' (Dan. 4:29-31). And Nebuchadnezzar became like an animal.

God had further lessons for Nebuchadnezzar, however. Here they are in Nebuchadnezzar's later confession:

'[God's] dominion is an eternal dominion;
    his kingdom endures from generation to generation.
All the peoples of the earth
    are regarded as nothing.
He does as he pleases
    with the powers of heaven
    and the peoples of the earth.
No one can hold back his hand
    or say to him: "What have you done?"'

(Dan. 4:34-35).

The cases of these four kings differ. With Pharaoh and Nebuchadnezzar God acted behind the scenes to bring them to their thrones. Yet even here there is variety. In Pharaoh's case God said nothing. In restoring Nebuchadnezzar, however, he announced what he would do. That was God's sovereignty in action.

In the cases of Saul and David God used human means, the work of Samuel. That too was the Lord's sovereign act. Sometimes God works one way, sometimes another. But whenever a political figure becomes prominent, God has done it for his own purposes. He raises up rulers, and he takes them down again, just as he wills.

We see too that *God controls the policies of the leaders that he raises to power.* We must not think that God puts kings in place and leaves their activities to chance. Far from it! The writer of Proverbs said, 'The king's heart is in the hand of the Lord; he directs it like a watercourse wherever he pleases' (Prov. 21:1). The picture is taken from irrigation. The farmer sends the water where he wants it to go by watercourses or irrigation canals. So the Lord directs the courses of the kings that he puts in place. This is a proverb, a generalization. It does not tell us what God has done with this or that king; it tells us how God deals with kings in general. Why does the king do what he does? Part of the answer is that he does it because the Lord wants it done.

We can see this illustrated in the Old Testament. The King of Assyria is a striking case in point. His story is found in Isaiah. We shall take it in little bites.

First, God speaks of sending the armies of Assyria against his rebellious people, Israel:

'Woe to the Assyrian, the rod of my anger,
    in whose hand is the club of my wrath!
I send him against a godless nation,
    I dispatch him against a people who anger me,
to seize loot and snatch plunder,
    and to trample them down like mud in the streets.
But this is not what he intends,
    this is not what he has in mind;
his purpose is to destroy,
    to put an end to many nations'

                                  (Isa. 10:5-7).

The main point is worth repeating: God is the Sender, the one who despatches Assyria. Is that true, when Assyria will plunder and loot and trample down women and children? Yes, it is true. The Lord sends Assyria on her mission.

But that is not all. Assyria will act for God. The army is a rod in God's hand. That is how closely God is involved. Even the club that the Assyrian soldier wields 'is the club of my wrath'. The King of Assyria sends his army to battle, but they do the work of the Lord! Of course, it is not the king's intention to serve the Lord. That is not what his troops want. Not at all! They aim to destroy, but the Lord sends them and uses them as he pleases.

Let's read further: 'When the Lord has finished all his work against Mount Zion and Jerusalem, he will say, "I will punish the king of Assyria for the wilful pride of his heart and the haughty look in his eyes. For he says:

'By the strength of my hand I have done this,
    and by my wisdom, because I have understanding.
I removed the boundaries of nations,
    I plundered their treasures;
    like a mighty one I subdued their kings.
As one reaches into a nest,
    so my hand reached for the wealth of nations;
as men gather abandoned eggs,
    so I gathered all the countries;
not one flapped a wing,
    or opened its mouth to chirp''''

                                 (Isa. 10:12-14).

'What a fine fellow I am!' said the King of Assyria. 'Look at all I've done. I've grabbed the nations of the world as men gather eggs. Come, admire my power and wisdom!' But the Lord saw things differently. He asked,

> 'Does the axe raise itself above him who swings it,
>   or the saw boast against him who uses it?
> As if a rod were to wield him who lifts it up,
>   or a club brandish him who is not wood!'
>
> (Isa. 10:15).

It would be ridiculous and impossible for an axe, a saw, a rod, or a club to exalt itself above the workman who uses it. Why, then, will the King of Assyria speak as if he were God? He is not God. He is not even independent of God. He is an instrument in God's hand. He carries out the policies of the Lord. It would be hard to find a stronger statement of God's sovereignty than this: God is the workman — Assyria, the tool!

That brings me to one final point about political leaders: *God gives them success or failure, just as it pleases him.* We may not like it, but the Lord may give little worldly success to a godly leader, and he may allow an ungodly king to succeed year after year. The career of Cyrus, King of Persia, illustrates this. He was God's own 'anointed' king even though he did not acknowledge the Lord. Listen to the Lord speaking to him:

> 'This is what the Lord says to his anointed,
>   to Cyrus, whose right hand I take hold of
> to subdue nations before him
>   and to strip kings of their armour,
> to open doors before him
>   so that gates will not be shut:
> I will go before you
>   and will level the mountains;
> I will break down gates of bronze
>   and cut through bars of iron.
> I will give you the treasures of darkness,
>   riches stored in secret places,
> so that you may know that I am the Lord,
>   the God of Israel, who summons you by name'
>
> (Isa. 45:1-3).

If we did not know better, we would have thought that these words were addressed to a righteous king in Judah. But no, these promises are given to a heathen king. God will walk hand in hand with Cyrus and will give him the treasures and riches that others will desperately seek to hide. Will this lead to the conversion of Cyrus? Apparently not, but it will serve the Lord's purposes. The passage goes on:

> 'For the sake of Jacob my servant,
>   of Israel my chosen,
> I summon you by name
>   and bestow on you a title of honour,
>   though you do not acknowledge me.
> I am the Lord, and there is no other;
>   apart from me there is no God.
> I will strengthen you,
>   though you have not acknowledged me,
> so that from the rising of the sun
>   to the place of its setting
> men may know that there is none besides me.
>   I am the Lord, and there is no other.
> I form the light and create darkness,
>   I bring prosperity and create disaster;
>   I the Lord, do all these things...
> I will raise up Cyrus in my righteousness:
>   I will make all his ways straight.
> He will rebuild my city
>   and set my exiles free,
> but not for a price or reward,
>   says the Lord Almighty'

(Isa. 45:4-7, 13).

God speaks here in general terms: he is the one who produces prosperity and disaster (v.7). Then he focuses upon a specific case. He will make Cyrus prosper and bring disaster on others, so that God's people will return to their land (v.13). The heathen king, Cyrus, will succeed, because God wants him to. His success will further the work of God.

If God gives success he also brings failure. Earlier we saw that the Lord raised Pharaoh to Egypt's throne. But he did more than that:

God caused Pharaoh's utter failure with Israel. When the Lord said, 'Let my people go' (Exod. 5:1), Pharaoh made up his mind to keep them. 'Who is the Lord, that I should obey him and let Israel go?' he asked, and he was foolish enough to add, 'I will not let Israel go' (Exod. 5:2). But God caused him to fail, even though Israel had no strength to compare with that of Pharaoh. The lesson is clear: God gives success or failure, just as it pleases him.

Does God control the acts of wicked men? Yes, he does. I have chosen ungodly kings as examples of how God acts. After all, ancient kings were the most powerful men of their day. Their wills were law. They did as they pleased. More than most men, they could defy the desires of others. If God controlled them, we should not be surprised if he controlled lesser men as well, and that is what we find.

The book of Proverbs says, 'In his heart a man plans his course, but the Lord determines his steps' (Prov. 16:9). That is God's way with men. Remember that proverbs are generalizations. They do not describe exceptional or unusual cases. Men quote proverbs to show what is generally or always true, and God gave his book of Proverbs for the same reason. Wicked men may boast of their independence from God. They may claim to be the masters of their fates and the captains of their souls, but it does not matter; all their plans are under the eye of God. Often he allows them to do as they please. They may curse and mock him. They may arrogantly brag. But in the end they carry out his purposes. The steps they take are ordered by the Lord. Men cannot make him forsake his throne. God remains King, even over the ungodly.

Note

1. I have taken 'I have raised you up' here to mean, 'I have raised you to the throne.' Some have thought that the words mean: 'I have brought you into existence for this very purpose...' That would be an even more emphatic statement of God's sovereignty.

5.
More evidence of God's kingship

We have been looking at a number of direct statements in Scripture
that tell us that God rules and have seen that his purposes are always
carried out. The Bible makes the point repeatedly: God is on the
throne. An ancient prophet once asked, 'When disaster comes to a
city, has not the Lord caused it?' (Amos 3:6). He expected his
readers to answer, 'Yes'. Even calamity comes from the King of
heaven. Wicked men and unhappy events work his will. There are
no exceptions.

Along with these *direct* statements, God's Word also contains
indirect evidence of the Lord's kingship. Much that Scripture tells
us implies that God rules everywhere, even when it does not say it
in so many words.

Take prophecy, for instance, the foretelling of coming events.[1]
How do we understand it? Do we think of God looking into the
future to see what will happen and then passing on what he sees?
That view is surely false. Remember how often God speaks of what
he will do in the future. He describes himself as the one

'who carries out the words of his servants
    and fulfils the predictions of his messengers,
who says of Jerusalem, "It shall be inhabited,"
    of the towns of Judah, "They shall be built,"
    and of their ruins, "I will restore them,"
who says to the watery deep, "Be dry,
    and I will dry up your streams,"
who says of Cyrus, "He is my shepherd

and will accomplish all that I please;
he will say of Jerusalem, 'Let it be rebuilt,'
and of the temple, 'Let its foundations be laid'"'
(Isa. 44:26-28).

Certainly in this case the Lord is not passive, merely telling what he foresees. Not at all! He will make the future what it will be. He himself will carry out the predictions that he puts into his prophets' mouths. He will work in places as diverse as the land of Judah and the heart of a heathen king. This is a fair sample of what we find all through the Bible. Here we read of the future mainly in literal terms. Elsewhere we find figurative language, as in the book of Revelation. The form varies, but the fact remains: God and his agents are the chief actors in the prophetic future. Throughout history God remains King. Men and angels do what pleases him.

There is one kind of prophecy that, more than any other, shows God's kingship over history. I am thinking of *typology*. First let me explain what I mean by typology, and then I will show how closely it is tied up with God's rule.

What is typology?[2] Typology is a method of Bible study that finds likenesses, intended by God, between a person or a thing in an earlier portion of God's revelation and another person or thing in a later portion. The key idea is this: the likeness is not merely in the mind of the reader, but was built into history by God himself. A type is more than an illustration; it is a model that the later person or thing will reproduce. It may be startling, but it is not arbitrary. It does not ignore the historical meaning of the older text. Rather, it builds on it.

An example or two will help make this clear. Almost as soon as we open the New Testament we meet Matthew quoting the Old Testament in an unusual way. Here is the background for our first quotation. Herod has been frustrated by the wise men or magi from the East. He had hoped to find out from them exactly where he could lay his hands on the newborn 'king'. But the wise men did not come back to Jerusalem to report to him on their findings, and, of course, he was angry. At the same time an angel of the Lord told Joseph to take his family into Egypt to stay out of Herod's way. Matthew says, 'So [Joseph] got up, took the child and his mother during the night and left for Egypt, where he stayed until the death of Herod. And so was fulfilled what the Lord had said through the prophet: "Out of

Egypt I called my son'" (Matt. 2:14-15). Here Matthew claims that
Scripture was fulfilled by what happened. Let's see what he means.

'Out of Egypt I called my son' comes from Hosea 11:1. The
entire verse reads, 'When Israel was a child, I loved him, and out of
Egypt I called my son.' This looks like a straightforward statement
of fact, and that is what it is. It is not a prediction in the usual sense
at all. The verse looks back at Israel's exodus from Egypt and traces
it up to the love of God. It says nothing about the future and nothing
about the Lord Jesus. Yet Matthew says it was 'fulfilled'. Is
Matthew confused? No, he saw the meaning of Hosea 11:1 as well
as we do. It is one of those verses that anyone with a slight
knowledge of Israel's past could not fail to grasp. As an Israelite,
Matthew knew exactly what Hosea was saying. So when Matthew
says that this scripture was 'fulfilled', he is using 'fulfilled' in a
different way. He is using it typically. Israel's exodus from Egypt
was a type, a picture, of the experience Jesus would later pass
through. By treating this as a fulfilment of Scripture, and not simply
as an illustration, Matthew tells us that God planned this
resemblance. These two moments in history, separated by more than
a thousand years, belong together.

But there is more to it than that. The first event, Israel's exodus
from Egypt, was actually planned with the second event, Christ's
return from Egypt, in mind. The fulfilment of a type is always more
important than the type itself. The fulfilment determines what the
type will be like, and not vice versa. Israel's release from Egypt was
an act of God that looked towards the coming of Christ. It was
Christ's future coming, including his return from Egypt, that made
Israel's release from Egypt meaningful. Or we could say that
Christ's coming was the end, and Israel's exodus was a means to that
end. That tells us that God not only ruled over the acts of Jesus' life
to make them come out as they did, but he ruled over the events of
the exodus in the same way. This parallel between Israel's
experience and the life of Christ shows God's kingship in both acts.

Even that is not all. Remember that these two events were more
than a thousand years apart. Is it possible that God relaxed his rule
in the years between them? Judge for yourself. If he had done so, it
is more than likely that there would have been no family of Judah
from which Christ could have come, no nation of Egypt for him to
visit, or no nation of Israel to which he might return. After all, the
Hittites, the Assyrians and many other peoples disappeared from

history during those years — why not the Egyptians, the nation of Israel, or the tribe of Judah? What force controlled their destinies? The answer has to be 'God'!

Typology, then, implies God's control throughout Israel's history, a control that extends to the nation of Egypt as well. As with prophecy in general, typology cannot be explained by God's mere foresight of events. More is needed. That 'more' is his hand in all that happens.

Let's look at one more example. When the Lord brought Israel out of Egypt he gave them a system of sacrifices. Those sacrifices showed that sin was no small thing and that Israel needed to be reconciled to God. But, beyond that, the sacrifices looked forward to Christ. They were types, or pictures, of the coming death of the Lord Jesus. The writer of Hebrews makes this point through much of his book. He speaks of Jesus as the perfect High Priest, who offers his own blood in sacrifice for sin. When he writes that 'It is impossible for the blood of bulls and goats to take away sins' (Heb. 10:4), he lets us know that the Old Testament sacrifices looked beyond their own power to the death of Christ. Would God have created a sacrificial system that did not work? Surely not! Why then did he tell Israel to offer bulls and goats? He did it first of all to picture Christ's obedience, by which 'we have been made holy through the sacrifice of the body of Jesus Christ once for all' (Heb. 10:10).

We see this truth, that the Old Testament sacrifices were pictures or types of the work of Christ, in much of Scripture. Isaiah says,

'He was pierced for our transgressions,
    he was crushed for our iniquities;
the punishment that brought us peace was upon him,
    and by his wounds we are healed.
We all, like sheep, have gone astray,
    each of us has turned to his own way;
and the Lord has laid on him
    the iniquity of us all.
He was oppressed and afflicted,
    yet he did not open his mouth;
he was led like a lamb to the slaughter . . . .
Yet it was the Lord's will to crush him and cause him to
    suffer,

>   and though the Lord makes his life a guilt offering,
> he will see his offspring and prolong his days,
>   and the will of the Lord will prosper in his hand'

>   (Isa. 53:5-7,10).

To Isaiah, the Servant of Yahweh died as a 'guilt offering' in the place of sinners. In that way he was just like a lamb led to the slaughter.

The New Testament takes up this theme as well. John the Baptist points to Jesus with these words: 'Look, the Lamb of God, who takes away the sin of the world!'(John 1:29). The Lord Jesus fulfils the role of the dying Old Testament lamb. Paul makes this even more explicit. 'For Christ,' he writes, 'our Passover lamb, has been sacrificed' (1 Cor. 5:7). Why could they say these things? Because God is Lord of history. He not only created history, he rules it from beginning to end.

So prophecy in general and typology both show that God controls history. I have called this indirect evidence of God's rule. Is there more such evidence? Yes, indeed. Here is a verse of Scripture cherished by most Christians. We will remind ourselves of what it says and then work through its implications: 'And we know that God causes all things to work together for good to those who love God, to those who are called according to his purpose' (Rom. 8:28, NASB).[3]

First let us look at the context. This verse comes at the end of a section of Romans that shows us our weakness and helplessness. Paul speaks of the Christian's sufferings (Rom. 8:18). He mentions our groanings (Rom. 8:23). And he makes clear that we do not know how to help ourselves. Surely we ought to cry out to God, but Paul says, 'We do not know what we ought to pray for' (Rom. 8:26). This is not a pretty picture.

Yet Paul does not leave you without hope, if you are a believer. He gives you two encouragements. First he tells you that God himself, God the Holy Spirit, prays for you. As soon as you hear that, you know that God will do you good. But are you ready for what he says next? In verse 28 he assures you that God works everything together for your good. It is one thing for God to do you good, but when Paul tells you that 'all things' do you good, what can you do but bow your head in adoration?

Now think of what Romans 8:28 involves. It confirms all that we have learned about God's kingship. Paul did not write this with his head in the sand. He knew that Christians are likely to be pushed around by all kinds of evil forces. Some of them will be what we call 'natural evils', things like fires and floods. Some of them will be evil men, and some of them will be demonic. At times we shall be tempted to say, 'Surely these things cannot do me good, can they?' 'Yes,' says Paul, 'they can and they will!' And Paul speaks by inspiration of the Spirit of God. No wonder he asks a few verses later, 'If God is for us, who can be against us?' God's sovereignty was not new to Paul when he wrote that sentence, but recalling it rekindled the flame of enthusiasm for God's kingship in his heart. We feel it as we read his words.

It is possible to lose some of the sense of wonder by dissecting truth, but I want to take that risk and go a step further. Up till now we have thought of Romans 8:28 as it bears on isolated men and women. I have been saying, 'Look at this incident in your experience and look at that incident, and see that God is making each of them do you good.' But, of course, there are no isolated men and women. There are no isolated incidents. We do not live in a vacuum. You and I are parts of a great web of events and circumstances that hang together, that are related to each other. These circumstances have their causes. Can those causes, then, be out of the control of God? Surely not! Beyond that, the things that happen to us become the causes of still other things. Every effect that God produces in his people is the source of much else. Like a pebble dropped in a quiet pool, God's work sends the ripples of his influence outward in widening circles. Are those ripples out of his control? How could they be? Many of them will touch the lives of still other believers, and in every case they will do his people good.

We might pursue this illustration further by asking how many things happen to each believer in a day, and by multiplying that number by the number of believers in the world. The result would be staggering. But even then we would not be done. What about other believers of other ages? We would have to add them to our calculations, wouldn't we? Right now we are feeling the effects of the writings of Paul, a Christian of 2,000 years ago. And due to the sovereign work of God, it does us good!

In this chapter we have been seeing evidence of God's kingship as it appears indirectly in the Scriptures. We considered prophecy and typology and saw how they show God's comprehensive control of his world. Prophecy does not tell us what God sees by peeping into the future, but rather what God intends to do. Typology is a special case of prophecy. It is prophecy presented in events rather than in words and it too requires a sovereign God.

Finally we looked at a single verse of Scripture, Romans 8:28. Here also we saw the King at work, and much more. We saw that if each thing works for the good of believers, and if nothing is an exception, then God must have his hand upon every event and circumstance in our lives. And we cannot stop there. Our lives are interwoven with the lives of other men. The events that come our way are set in motion by both men and angels, godly and ungodly. The world is a network of causes and effects. Our minds reel when we begin to trace out the causes and effects of a single incident. In fact, it is impossible for us to do so. Yet if these things were not in the hand of God, some event might sneak into our lives to undo us. It would no longer be true that *all* things do us good. But it is true. Why? Because God is King in every event and circumstance of life.

Notes

1. Of course, prophecy is not only foretelling the future. It serves many purposes, including encouragement and rebuke.
2. I have been helped in this section by S. Lewis Johnson, *The Old Testament in the New*, Zondervan, Grand Rapids, 1980, especially chapters 4 and 5. Johnson defines typology as 'the study of spiritual correspondences between persons, events and things within the historical framework of God's special revelation' (p.55).
3. The NIV has 'In all things God works for good...' This might suggest that Paul means: 'In every situation there is something that God is doing for the believer's good.' But Paul's idea is much more comprehensive than that. There is nothing in the Greek text to justify the NIV's use of 'in'.

6.
The God of purpose

Let's see where we have been so far. We have been talking about God's kingship or sovereignty over circumstances and events. I said in chapter 2 that we would look at this in three ways. First, we would examine the *direct* statements of Scripture about God's control of his world. We have done that. Second, we would look at some *indirect* evidence that demands his control. In the last chapter we did that. In both cases we took a mere sampling from Scripture. There is much more evidence of God's sovereignty in the Bible, both direct and indirect. Now we come to the third line of argument, the evidence suggested by what the Bible tells us about the character of God.

When we want to speak of what God is like, we must let God's Word take us by the hand. I do not suppose that any Christian will argue with that. It seems obvious to all of us. Why, then, do I need to say it? Because our ideas of God are so basic that they cannot easily be changed. That is as it should be. If I have come to God through Christ, my grasp of God's character cannot have been entirely faulty. I have learned precious truth about God that I must not lose hold of. But to change the way I view God, even in a small way, will throw much else that I believe out of adjustment. Can I stand that kind of revision in what I believe? That is a serious question, and it is not one I want to grapple with unless God's Word makes me do so.

We have already seen, however, how new truth affects our view of God. If you have followed what I have been saying about God's kingship up to this point, your ideas of God have no doubt been stretching and expanding as we have gone along. That is the way we grow and develop in our knowledge of God's Word, isn't it? We bring the ideas that we have gleaned from Scripture to each new passage that we read and study. In turn, the new passage modifies our old understanding ever so slightly, and we move on. Then we repeat the process; we do it over and over again. That 'revision' I was talking about a moment ago is always going on, if we are being honest with Scripture. What I say next will continue the process and should help us to grow further in our understanding of God.

I want us to look at God as the *God of purpose*. To grasp what that means we shall look first at two of God's attributes: his wisdom and knowledge. But we need to start by seeing what the phrase 'the God of purpose' means.

We may mean one of two things when we call God 'the God of purpose'. We may mean, first, that God has purpose when he acts. We have already seen that repeatedly. We have looked at his purposes with Job and Joseph, with the Assyrians and Israel. It is clear that God has purposes in what he does. No one could doubt that, but it does not get us very far. It is really just another way of saying that God is a person (or three persons in one). All persons generally act with purpose when they act. God is no exception.

We call God 'the God of purpose' because he has a single purpose, or a single set of purposes, that he pursues through all of history.

We are not like that. Our goals change. Our purposes often alter within a brief lifetime. Ask a boy what he hopes to be when he grows up. 'I want to be a pilot,' he says at one stage of his development, or 'I want to be a fireman.' These are serious purposes *at the time,* but most boys soon outgrow them. When the boy becomes a man the kind of goal may change. The answer to the question, 'What do you want to be?' may be 'I want to be successful' or 'I want to be well known.' Let this same boy or man come to Christ and his purposes will change again, more radically than ever. Even then he will daily suffer from conflict within himself about what goals he will pursue at a given moment. We are not 'persons of purpose' in the way God is. We do not have a single purpose or set of purposes that we faithfully pursue throughout life. Why not? In part, the answer is that we lack the knowledge and wisdom of God.

What would you need in order to form and consistently follow the same goals through the whole of your life? You would have to know everything. Suppose there was one fact in all the world that you did not know. That fact, when you finally stumbled upon it, might be the very thing that would undo your plans and make you change them. But, of course, there are billions of facts that you don't know. The same is true of me. That is why our purposes change and why we are sometimes at cross-purposes with ourselves.

The Lord, on the other hand, has all knowledge. He is omniscient, to use the theological term. 'Nothing in all creation is hidden from God's sight' (Heb. 4:13). 'His understanding has no limit' (Ps. 147:5). He is also all-wise. That means that he knows how to make the best use of all his knowledge. Wisdom is that kind of knowledge that tells a person what goals to choose and how to reach the goals he chooses. Now God has wisdom to perfection. Paul calls God's wisdom 'the manifold wisdom of God' (Eph. 3:10). By a daring figure he assures us that 'The foolishness of God is wiser than man's wisdom'! (1 Cor. 1:25).

Does this truth about God's wisdom and knowledge have anything to do with God's kingship, his sovereignty? Yes, it has a great deal to do with it.

The point at which all Christians have a problem with God's kingship is the entry of sin into the world. Here, if anywhere, we would like to say that things got out of hand. Here, if ever, we would like to believe that God did not have control. This is the point where we would like to lay aside the doctrine of the sovereignty of God. But can we do so? Not if we believe that God knows all things. Let me explain why.

Someone could say, 'Well, of course, God knew that men might fall when he made them. He gave them free will, so he had to reckon with that possibility.' Much more might be said along the same lines. But here is the important point: God knew much more than that men might fall. He created man knowing that man *certainly would* fall. That was not a fact God learned later. The God who knows all things knew, before he created Adam, that Adam would rebel against his Maker. But God chose to create Adam knowing certainly that he would fall. We cannot deny this unless we think that there are some things that God does not know.

But now suppose we ask the question: 'Was it wise to create man under these circumstances?' Or we could put it this way: 'Did God have some purpose in creating a man that he knew would fall?' If we answer, 'No,' we have denied the wisdom of God. If we answer,

'Yes,' we have said that even the Fall serves the purposes of the King! God's sovereignty appears in the most unlikely place, in the fall of man.

Let's turn back to people like ourselves for a moment. Does a wise man allow things to go wrong, when he can do something about them? Not usually, though there may be times when even a wise man will not know what to do, and times when he will let things go, hoping for the best. But does God act this way? The answer is plain, isn't it? God knows what to do at all times. And he knows what the outcome will be, so he does not 'hope for the best'.

But perhaps someone says, 'Surely God might let some little thing happen for which there was no purpose. That's what we do, after all.' But when we act like that we reveal our lack of wisdom! Anyway, even if God did sometimes do that, what then? It would still not help us with the fall of man. Was the fall of man 'some little thing'? Surely not! It was an enormous crime with far-reaching effects. Yet it was foreseen by the all-knowing God. His wisdom allowed it. There is only one way to explain the Fall without denying the knowledge and wisdom of God: we must admit that it served some great end. In other words, in the Fall as in all else, we are face to face with the purpose and sovereignty of God. The two things go hand-in-hand. They follow from the knowledge and wisdom of God.

We shall see the necessity of God's control if we look at others of his attributes as well. In a moment I will take up God's holiness and his power. But first a word of caution. As I wrote in my book, *A Vision for Missions*, 'Anyone who thinks about it will realize that God's person cannot be divided up as neatly as this implies. You cannot do that with any person. You cannot separate a man's character into neat compartments. You can talk about his loves and his hatreds, his envy and his desire, his wisdom and his power, but when you have finished you are left with but one person looked at in many ways.

'This is even more true of God. In God there are no inner contradictions. God is one harmonious whole. His [various attributes] are, after all, just himself looked at from different sides. That is why we cannot fix the number of God's attributes. It depends on how you look at him... What we are after is to know God, that we may worship him. The divisions we make are just a way to that goal.'[1]

We shall need to keep that in view as we talk about God's holiness and power.

God's wisdom and knowledge lead him to act in a sovereign manner. So also does his moral character, his consistent stance towards sin and righteousness. We have seen that God uses even sin to serve his purposes. The fall of man, with all the wickedness it brought forth, was not outside the purpose and control of God. But the Bible teaches that God is holy. He hates sin. He loves righteousness.

When we try to grasp what this means we see that we have to think within two limits. First, we know it does not mean that God will never allow sin in the world. That is clear. Sin exists. It is all around us. But if God's holiness means anything then our thinking is limited in another direction. We cannot think that God can allow any and every amount of sin in his universe. If he did that, even without personally sinning, he would be indifferent to sin. His holiness would be largely a name. It would have little content.

Where is the middle ground between these two limits, the presence of sin and God's hatred of it? It lies in allowing exactly the amount of sin that will further the purposes of God, and no more. Any less than that would be unwise; any more would be unholy. Now when we say that God limits sin to just the amount and variety that works his will, we are talking about the kingship, the sovereignty of God.

How detailed will the sovereignty that limits sin have to be? If we ask how much sin there is in the world, we will have our answer. If sin were as infrequent as the appearance of Halley's Comet it might not seem to require much control; but sin is involved in everything man does. All that natural men do is sinful. As Paul says, 'The mind of sinful man is death ... the sinful mind is hostile to God. It does not submit to God's law, nor can it do so. Those controlled by the sinful nature cannot please God' (Rom. 8:6-8). To please God is to act righteously. To defy him is to sin; and defying God is all that a natural man can do.

That means that the control of a natural man cannot be an occasional work — much less the control of *all* natural men! God must be King, *and act as King*, at all times. If he does not, needless sin will occur, and needless sin is not consistent with the holiness of God.

That is not all. Christians sin too. John warned believers, 'If we

claim to be without sin, we deceive ourselves' (1 John 1:8). So
Christians need control also. God must be King among his own
people, or they will produce still more sin that has no purpose.
Again, that would be inconsistent with God's holiness. What will he
do? God's holiness demands that he assert his sovereign rights over
his world. Only lack of power could keep him from doing so. But
God has all power; he is omnipotent. 'Is anything too hard for the
Lord?' (Gen. 18:14). No, nothing. He is the 'Lord God *Almighty*'
(Rev 19:6). His *might* extends to *all*. It reaches to every person and
to every thing. His wisdom and knowledge and holiness and power
combine to work his purposes in the world. What God is makes him
'the God of purpose'. Indeed, we may think of 'purpose' as one of
the attributes of God.

Reference
1. T. Wells, *A Vision for Missions,* p.43.

Part III

God's moral kingship and his kingship in the new creation

7.
What is God's moral kingship?

I have been saying that God rules over all the circumstances and events of life. That is a large claim, much too large for me to make on my own, but it is the Bible's claim. God is King over all that we see and hear.

That raises a question. Does it seem to you that I have left no room for God to be King in new ways, ways in which he is not already exercising his kingship? 'After all,' someone might say, 'if every circumstance and event is what it is because God wants it that way, what else is left? Isn't that the same as saying that everything, without exception, is the work of God? God is King in every sense, and that's that?'

You may be surprised at my answer. While God retains his *right to act* whenever and wherever he pleases, I do not hold that God *acts* as King in every sense. The Bible does not teach that. It teaches something quite different.

Think with me of this passage, here given in the familiar words of the Authorized, or King James, Version: 'Thy kingdom come. Thy will be done in earth, as it is in heaven' (Matt. 6:10) What have we here? Clearly it is a prayer that God would exercise his will and act as King in a new way. This prayer shows that there is some important sense in which God does not act as sovereign. I say 'some *important* sense' because this is not taken from just any prayer. It comes from that model prayer that we call 'the Lord's Prayer', a prayer that is concerned with the most weighty topics of all, such as God's glory and his care for us. Right in the middle of that prayer we have the request that God would assert control. What can that mean?

The key lies in that little phrase: '… as it is in heaven'. Jesus tells us that God's will is done differently in heaven, and he gives the reason. In some sense God rules in heaven in a way that he does not yet rule here on earth. We are to pray for his rule to be exercised here in the same way as it is there.

What is missing here on earth? One of the things that are missing is what I have called 'moral sovereignty'. By that I mean that in this world God does not usually act as King over *the motives of men* in the sense that he gets his work done without making men have godly reasons for what they do. They do his will outwardly. They produce circumstances and events that further God's purposes — that is clear. But he does not make all fallen men obedient on the inside. Outwardly men and Satan do things that God wants done, but inwardly they have no desire to please God any further than doing what God wants happens to fit in with their own plans and goals. In other words, Satan and fallen men aim to serve themselves, not God. The fact that what they do works out God's purposes is merely an accident as far as they are concerned. It is not obedience to God. [1]

We can see, then, that there is a vast area, that of men's motives, that God could rule if he cared to do so. In one sense God already rules men's motives. After all, men have only the motives that God determined to allow for his own purposes. But there is a different, higher kind of rule over the motives of men. It is a rule that *makes men's motives godly*. To grasp what this rule or moral sovereignty is, you must go back with me to the fall of man.

When God made man, he made him holy. Man delighted to do the will of God. We know this because man was created to have fellowship with God and to put his heart into the tasks that the Lord laid out for him. But there can be no fellowship with God and no heartfelt obedience apart from holiness. Man's heart and will were at peace with God's commands.

The job that God gave man to do was clear, and it was important. Man was to be prime minister over God's world. The earth and its animals and its fruits were a trust. They were God's, but he gave them into the hands of man to be used in whatever ways he would make plain from time to time. Man and the world were a pair. Each was made by God and for God, but they were also made for each other. There were three parties to God's arrangement: God himself, man his creature, and the world God had made. And there was harmony throughout. Man stood between God and earth and was at peace with both.

The point that we must not miss is this: man had not yet insisted on deciding for himself what is right and wrong. The moment he did so, harmony in both directions was broken. As far as man could tell at that moment, it was broken for ever. The first sin was much more than a mistake or an error of judgement. It was an act of rebellion, as all sin is, with enormous consequences.

First, *God was no longer King in the moral sense.* We have seen that God kept control of circumstances and events, but he did so without causing the motives of men to be godly. In that way he let men have their own way. [2]

Second, *man no longer held the earth in trust for God.* We can see that man took the reins into his own hands. We also know from Scripture that at the same time he gave up those reins to Satan. He did this without realizing what he had done. At his creation man was the willing tool of God. Now he became the unwitting tool of Satan. Man may boast of his freedom to do as he pleases, but in fact he does as Satan pleases. The Bible is quite plain on this point. Satan is now 'the ruler of the kingdom of the air, the spirit who is now at work in those who are disobedient' (Eph. 2:2). He is also called 'the god of this age', who 'has blinded the minds of unbelievers' (2 Cor. 4:4).

These remarkable statements are the Lord's own words about Satan. They are not mine. They are not even Satan's. They come from Paul, writing by the inspiration of God. We must not misunderstand them, of course. They do not mean that Satan has any right to rule in this world. No, he is a usurper. God retains the right of kingship. It is his; nothing could take that from him. But the fact remains that *in a moral sense*, Satan rules; that is, he rules the motives of men. And in that way he keeps man from holding this world as a trust for God.

A third result follows from man's sin: *the earth no longer willingly serves man.* The ground gives up its crops reluctantly. The wild beasts start up at the sound of man's voice, not in happy obedience to his will, but to flee him or to fling themselves on him in deadly combat. With anguish in his heart and sweat on his face, man seeks to gain a living from this earth. The harmony is gone. In its place is a fight to the death between man and his old ally, the world.

We have, then, these three changes:

1. God no longer King in a moral sense;

2. The earth no longer held in trust for God;
3. Man and the world around him in disharmony.

You can see that it took me just three lines to list these things, but we must not measure their importance by counting the lines. I can hardly imagine greater revolutions than these.

Of course, we must not think that these changes took the Lord by surprise. Not at all! They were part of his plan. It looks very much as if these shifts in power opened the way for God to reveal the aspects of his character that he could only show in the presence of sin, qualities like mercy and grace. Isn't that what Paul tells us in Romans? Look at this: 'But where sin increased, grace increased all the more, so that, just as sin reigned in death, so also grace might reign through righteousness to bring eternal life through Jesus Christ our Lord' (Rom. 5:20-21). Or again, 'For God has bound all men over to disobedience so that he may have mercy on them all. (Rom. 11:32). In other words, Adam and Eve, choosing freely, set the stage for God's great acts of redemption. No wonder Paul added these words of intense astonishment:

> 'Oh, the depths of the riches of the wisdom and knowledge of
>   God!
>   How unsearchable his judgements,
>   and his paths beyond tracing out!'

> (Rom. 11:33).

What else could he say?

But to get back to Adam and Eve: the day they sinned God had a ruined human race on his hands and a world that was out of harmony with the race that he had set over it. In fact, God himself brought about this discord between man and the earth. To Adam God said,

> 'Cursed is the ground because of you;
>   through painful toil you will eat of it
>   all the days of your life.
> It will produce thorns and thistles for you,
>   and you will eat the plants of the field.
> By the sweat of your brow
>   you will eat your food

until you return to the ground,
    since from it you were taken;
for dust you are
    and to dust you will return'

(Gen. 3:17-19).

This left creation in need of a new humanity, a new earth and a new bond between the two of them. The old alliance was gone, and it stayed 'gone'. Centuries later Paul summed up the relationship between man and his world in Romans 8:19-22: 'The creation waits in eager expectation for the sons of God to be revealed. For the creation was subjected to frustration, not by its own choice, but by the will of the one who subjected it, in hope that the creation itself will be liberated from its bondage to decay and brought into the glorious freedom of the children of God. We know that the whole creation has been groaning as in the pains of childbirth right up to the present time.' In a startling figure Paul makes creation cry out with birthpangs as it hungrily longs for God to renew mankind!

Now here is the point we need to grasp: the curse that hurled man and earth apart, and set them into a kind of competition, had a moral cause. God pronounced the curse because Adam did wrong. The act that puts them back together will have to be moral as well. It will be an act of power, but not just any act of power. It will re-establish God as man's King in a moral sense, causing men to adopt God's own attitudes towards good and evil, right and wrong. God's sovereignty will be a moral sovereignty. His kingdom then will have come in the fullest sense. His will shall 'be done in earth as it is in heaven', and its effect will be to produce harmony between the new humanity and the new earth for ever.

Notes

1. Here is the point I am making summed up by the theologian John Murray: 'There is danger that we view ... obedience mechanically or quantitatively, as if it consisted merely in the sum-total of formal acts of obedience. But an act externally conformed to God's requirements may not be one of obedience. To be an act of obedience, the whole dispositional complex of motive, direction, and purpose must be in conformity to the divine will.' *Collected Writings,* vol. II , Banner of Truth Trust, 1977, p. 152.

2. From this point on, whenever I say that God was no longer King, this (and only this) is what I mean: after the Fall God did not make the motives of all men to be godly.

8.
Enter Jesus Christ

We have already seen that God is King. A king is a ruler, and ruling is what God does all the time. He rules so widely and so powerfully that every circumstance and event that we see, or hear of, serves his purposes. Nothing happens that does not help along the work of God. It is impossible to say how God can do this, but that should not surprise us. We are creatures, not the Creator. We are men, not God.

We have also seen that there remains a sense in which God does not rule. He does not make the motives of men to be godly motives. He does not exert moral kingship everywhere and at all times. We pray that he may do that here in the earth, but he has not yet answered that prayer and we do not know when he will do so.

What he has told us is this. First, that day is coming. Second, he will bring it about through the work of his Son, whom he has named heir of all things in heaven and earth. God's Son, Jesus Christ, will be King. Indeed, he is King already. He told his early followers, 'All authority in heaven and on earth has been given to me' (Matt. 28:18). Yet there is no rivalry and no inconsistency between the kingship of God and the sovereignty of Christ. Christ is the instrument by whom God's kingdom comes. Our next task, then, is to try to find out what this means.

I said earlier that in the beginning God made man his prime minister. Man was to rule all the creatures around him. He was to be a sort of king under God. The rest of the creation was to obey and serve man; and it did so until man rebelled against God. The first man, Adam, was much more a king in this world than any of the kings that have lived and ruled since. Then he fell, and the Fall left him, and all of us who have come after him, struggling with the creation to subdue it and to gain a living from it.

However, God had a plan. He planned first to undo the effects of the Fall. That meant three things:

1. God would again be King in a moral sense.
2. The earth would again be held in trust for God.
3. Man and the world would live in harmony once more.

But God went even further: he decided to do these things in such a way that the new creation would be far more resplendent than the old, even before the Fall. That is where Jesus Christ, his Son, comes into the picture. One man had failed, and all men with him. But what if another came in his place and succeeded where Adam and Eve had fallen down on the job? And what if this 'last Adam' was able to form a new race of men like himself? Then the way would be clear to put men and creation back into a working harmony. That, in brief, is what God planned to do, on a scale that man could not have dreamed of then, a scale that we can only glimpse even now.

God's first step, then, was to prepare the world for the coming of his Son. One way in which he did this was to promise his coming. He told of the day when earth would be renewed, and he tied that promise to his Servant-Son:

'Here is my servant, whom I uphold,
    my chosen one in whom I delight;
I will put my Spirit on him
    and he will bring justice to the nations.
He will not shout or cry out,
    or raise his voice in the streets.
A bruised reed he will not break,
    and a smouldering wick he will not snuff out.
In faithfulness he will bring forth justice;
    he will not falter or be discouraged
till he establishes justice on earth.
    In his law the islands will put their hope'

(Isa. 42:1-4).

There you have it, a world unlike any world we have ever set foot in, a world of justice ruled by a King known for his gentleness and meekness! That is the promise. And all the while God allowed the wickedness of men and nations to grow, so that his triumph would be the more glorious.

As long years went by, God fanned the flames of man's longing with repeated promises of the coming King. Through his prophets God spoke of the 'Prince of Peace' whose government would last for ever (Isa. 9:6-7) and the 'righteous Branch, a King who will reign wisely' (Jer. 23:5). Even though Israel often despised God's promises and forgot their Maker, he encouraged his people with this: 'Afterwards the Israelites will return and seek the Lord their God and David their king. They will come trembling to the Lord and to his blessings in the last days' (Hosea 3:4).

At last, 'When the time had fully come, God sent his Son ...' (Gal. 4:4). God was as good as his promise. The Branch from David's line came as Jesus of Nazareth.

In the earthly life of Jesus we begin to see what we mean by God's moral kingship. From the time that Adam fell until the Lord Jesus came into the world, there had never been a man or woman who did not sin against God — not one! So the first thing that God did in sending his Son was to show us a man who was totally ruled by the will of God. 'My food,' Jesus once told his disciples, 'is to do the will of him who sent me and to finish his work' (John 4:34). Those were not mere words. The ecstasies and the agonies of his life had the same source, the will of his Father. Once he asked his enemies, 'Can any of you prove me guilty of sin?' (John 8:46). He knew they could not do so. He had no sin for men to ferret out. God was King in the life of Jesus of Nazareth. God's moral kingship was perfectly seen in him.

Yet the Lord Jesus was sorely tried; his was no cheap victory. He was given a heart and a mind to serve God, as Adam was. But he was bumped about and battered by temptation in a way that Adam and Eve never knew. Their collapse under the first stroke of temptation kept them from feeling the hammer blows that fell upon Christ. P. E. Hughes has written on Hebrews 4:15: 'His sinlessness meant that the temptations came to him with a sharpness far greater than is known to us whose minds and wills have become dull through frequent failures.' Someone once asked the question: 'Do you know the best way to get rid of temptation?' and answered it by saying, 'Give in, and it will go right away!' We know from sad experience how true that is. But Jesus never once took that way out. The writer of Hebrews expressed this most clearly: 'We have one who has been tempted in every way, just as we are — yet was without sin' (Heb. 4:15). God was King in the life of Jesus Christ each time Jesus faced a question of right or wrong. There were no exceptions.

That was the beginning. But God also planned to put the Lord Jesus at the head of a new race of men, a new humanity, so there was a good deal more for him to do. He had one new 'Adam', but his goal was to have millions, perhaps billions, 'a great multitude that no one could count' (Rev. 7:9). These new men and women would be like Jesus and would be the products of his work. Through him they would be adopted into the family of God. It is a staggering vision — a vision worthy of the true God.

There were two possible ways in which this could have been done: a simple way and a hard way. The simple way would have been to wipe out the old race of men completely and to start all over again. A single act of power would have achieved this and it would have been an act of justice as well. But God chose the hard way. He planned to make the new race out of the old race. Once more he would use his power, but he would bring his justice into play in a different way. Justice demanded the destruction of all the rebels against his authority, but — and here is what made this the 'hard' way — God planned to take the destruction of a vast number of them upon himself.

I do not want to take much time to explain how God did this. It is, of course, one of the best-known features of Christianity. But I have already said that it is by Jesus Christ that God would make this new world, and it is in the Lord Jesus that God took on himself the destruction and death that should have fallen on all the rebels. That is what the cross is all about. There we see God the Son bearing the curse of God's broken law: the curse that should have driven me (and every other Christian with me) right down into hell. He died there, 'the just for the unjust' (1 Peter 3:18, AV).

The effect of the cross was this: justice was satisfied. Christ died as a substitute for all whom God intended to save, and God was now free to exercise his kingly power to make the new race the way he wanted it to be. It would have been just to destroy us, but it could not be just to save us, unless someone bore the judgement against our sins. But Jesus Christ, the Son of God, did just that!

It is right here that many Christians seem to think we no longer need God's sovereignty. 'Fine,' they say, 'Christ has died and now it is up to men to decide what they will do with him. God has done his part, and now it's up to man to do his. We'll just see whether John over there will make Christ his Lord or not.' Well, I can tell you the answer to that right now: John won't do it!

9.
The new birth

I closed the last chapter by saying that an unconverted friend whom we will call 'John' will never make Jesus his Lord. There are two reasons I wrote that.

First, *Jesus Christ is already John's Lord.* The idea that somehow John is free from Jesus' lordship is false. I shall say more about that in a moment.

Secondly, according to the Bible, *John does not want Jesus.* John's mind and attitudes are hostile to the laws of heaven, those laws that the Lord Jesus loyally displayed in his own life here on earth. John and Jesus are fundamentally unlike and this dissimilarity goes to the very root of their beings. The last thing John will ever do on his own is to bow to the lordship of Jesus Christ. If anything is to be done with John, the kingly power of God will have to do it. There is as much need for the sovereignty of God in John's new creation as there was in his first creation — or, for that matter, in the creation of the world! Does this seem overstated? Let me show you why I have put it like this.

To begin with, John is dead. I know that he eats and drinks and plays and works and maybe even sometimes roars like the crowd in a football stadium to let the world know that he is alive. I can see that. I also know that he would feel outraged to be told that death has carried him away a captive, that what he calls life is only the empty husk of God's first gift to man. I understand all that. But the fact remains that John is dead. He is dead in the only way that can ultimately matter at all. He is dead towards God.

What do I mean by that? What is it, to be dead towards God? Here is an illustration from my earlier book, *Faith: the Gift Of God,* to show you what I am talking about. 'In a crowded room, buzzing with conversation, a young lady sits to one side, a distant look in her eyes. She has just received news. Her fiancé, thought to have been lost in battle, is alive and returning to her. What a reunion that will be! She can think of nothing else. She hears none of the small talk around her. A friend, waving from across the room, will not get her attention. She is insensible to her surroundings. They have no charms for her. To them she is dead.' Here is a woman utterly alive to the thought of her lover's return. And her breathless occupation with that one fact leaves her dead to all else. Dead? Yes, dead and 'buried in thought'!

If I had used a man in my illustration, he might have been our friend John. We are all like this, apart from the gracious power of God. Every sinner maintains his state of spiritual death by being intensely 'alive' to other things. Paul tells us plainly: 'As for you, you were dead in your trangressions and sins, in which you used to live when you followed the ways of this world and of the ruler of the kingdom of the air, the spirit who is now at work in those who are disobedient. All of us also lived among them at one time, gratifying the cravings of our sinful nature and following its desires and thoughts. Like the rest, we were by nature objects of wrath' (Eph. 2:1-3).

Can men be both dead and alive at the same time? Paul's answer is clear: every one of us was alive to sin and Satan before God intervened in our lives. There were all kinds of things that we wanted to do, and that Satan wanted us to do, and we did them. Paul calls them 'the ways of the world'. We may have spent a great deal of time, money and energy chasing the things that we thought would make us happy, and if anyone had come along to tell us that God was angry with us, that we were the objects of his wrath, we would have told that fellow to be on his way and to stop talking nonsense. God's wrath directed at us? Impossible! We didn't meddle with him and his enjoyment, and he had nothing to be angry about. We ran our little lives and let him do whatever he wanted with the heavens and the earth. Now that is precisely what the Bible means when it tells men that they are dead. It is not pretending that they have any lack of energy or plenty of directions in which to spend it. What it does mean is that not an ounce of that energy is spent for the glory of God, out of love for their Creator. Apart from God's grace, men are dead *towards God.*

How are dead men to be made alive? There is no answer to that question apart from the sovereignty of God. It is no use saying, 'All they have to do is choose God.' That is the one thing they will never do. Unless the Lord first gives them life, they will never choose him — not under any circumstances whatsoever.

Right here I have touched on the point that many modern Christians have not come to grips with. A natural man, a man dead towards God, will not choose God. The Bible gives a number of reasons why that is true.

First, *the natural man hates God.* I do not mean this or that natural man. No, the Scripture tells us that the whole world of natural men are enemies of God and of his law. Jesus said, 'He who is not with me is against me, and he who does not gather with me, scatters' (Luke 11:23). Perhaps we have heard these words so often that we no longer feel their force. Twice in this sentence the Lord Jesus shows the hostility between himself and what we like to call ordinary, decent people. Are such men and women really *against* Christ? Yes. Is there no neutral ground for them to stand on? No. They are 'against me', he says.

The second half of that sentence is even more striking. The enmity of the natural man, Jesus tells us, is not simply passive. It is not just the resistance of a heavy weight that needs to be moved out of the way. *It is active resistance.* While the Lord is busy gathering his sheep, the natural man is busy trying to drive them off. Or, if the figure is taken from harvest, while the Lord gathers in his grain, the natural man is seeking to scatter it to the four winds. Once again this is said of every natural man. The sides have been formed, and there is no neutral ground. The natural man has his feet planted on the wrong side. He fights in the wrong army. This is the hatred, the enmity, of the natural man.

This subject is so important that the Lord Jesus took it up during the last hours he had with his disciples before he was betrayed. 'If the world hates you,' he said, 'keep in mind that it hated me first. If you belonged to the world, it would love you as its own. As it is, you do not belong to the world, but I have chosen you out of the world. That is why the world hates you... He who hates me hates my Father as well... They have hated both me and my Father' (John 15:18-19, 23-24).

At first glance we might think that Jesus is speaking of particular enemies when he speaks of 'the world'. The Pharisees, for instance, were hounding him to death. Others also wanted him out of the way.

But that is not his point. He is speaking here of mankind at large, the world that these followers had been a part of. Once it had been their world, the orbit in which they moved. Jesus gives the reason why they no longer belonged to that world: 'I have chosen you out of the world.' What world? The world of lost mankind; the world of those who hate him. We may be sure that if these disciples were once a part of that world, we too were members of it. That goes also for our imaginary friend, John. No wonder John will not turn to Christ.

Following close on the heels of the natural man's hatred of God comes his estimate of God's truth: 'The man without the Spirit does not accept the things that come from the Spirit of God, for they are foolishness to him, and he cannot understand them, because they are spiritually discerned' (1 Cor. 2:14). We all know how slightly we pay attention to things that look like foolishness to us. That is Paul's point in this passage. He does not mean that every unconverted man laughs at the gospel, the story of the cross of Christ. Many lost men and women do not do that at all. But they have this in common: *they do not take the gospel seriously* where it begins to press on their own personal lives. They just cannot see how it means the end of their own good deeds as the way to God.

Of course, men have different ruses for laying the message aside. In Paul's day they fought off God's truth in two ways. If they were Jews they often rejected it on the ground that supernatural power would have to attend any word from God, and the story of a crucified criminal was about as far from supernatural power as you could get. If they were Greeks they said frankly, 'We know wisdom when we meet it, and this isn't it!'

Paul had a ready answer for these critics, but it was not one that they were likely to understand. 'Jews demand miraculous signs,' he writes, 'and Greeks look for wisdom, but we preach Christ crucified: a stumbling-block to Jews and foolishness to Gentiles, but to those whom God has called, both Jews and Greeks, Christ the power of God and the wisdom of God. For the foolishness of God is wiser than man's wisdom, and the weakness of God is stronger than man's strength' (1 Cor. 1:22-25)

Where Paul saw that it was the message itself that put men off, he made no long explanations. He knew that the natural man would see no use in what he preached, and he was wise enough to know that nothing that he could do would change that. 'For who among men knows the thoughts of a man except the man's spirit within him? In the same way no one knows the thoughts of God except the Spirit of God' (1 Cor. 2:11).

If a man has the Spirit of God he will hear and embrace the message. Otherwise he will not. 'My sheep listen to my voice,' said the Lord Jesus, 'I know them, and they follow me' (John 10:27). If a man does not recognize the voice of Jesus in the gospel, he will not respond. There is nothing that the preacher can do.

The Bible describes the condition of the sinner in yet a third way when it tells us that *he is blind*, or that he sits in darkness. It is only saying what everyone knows, that a blind man cannot see, but I have to emphasize it because we may read it repeatedly and still not grasp it. Paul tells us the state lost men are in: 'And even if our gospel is veiled, it is veiled to those who are perishing. The god of this age has blinded the minds of unbelievers, so that they cannot see the light of the gospel of the glory of Christ, who is the image of God' (2 Cor. 4:3-4). Men are blind. They 'cannot see the light of the gospel'. No wonder it is foolishness to them! Right here is our friend John's problem. He is unable to see 'the glory of Christ' when he hears the gospel. Men like John might adopt the words of Isaiah 53:2 about Christ: 'He had no beauty or majesty to attract us to him, nothing in his appearance that we should desire him.'

If men hate the Lord Jesus, if they find the gospel about him foolishness, and if they are blind to his attractiveness, we must not be surprised if they do not turn to him as Saviour and Lord. No, our friend John will never freely come to Christ without the sovereignty of God at work on his heart. What is the solution to John's dilemma? How is it possible that he may yet be saved? The answer lies in this fact: Jesus Christ is already John's Lord. That truth is the only hope for John's salvation. If John's Lord chooses to do so, he will take away the death and hatred and blindness of John's heart and replace them with life and faith and sight. Jesus Christ can do that, because he is Lord over all men, including John. And if the Lord Jesus does this for John, it will be a kingly act, an act of pure sovereignty. John, you see, is in the hands of Jesus Christ.

For many years I rejected this solution to John's dilemma. If you had asked me how John could be saved I would have said, 'John must exercise his free will. Christ has done his part, and now John must do his.' Why would I have said that? Because I did not take seriously the fact that John was dead towards God and blind to the glory of Christ. Beyond that, I failed to look closely at what the Scripture says about the cure for his deadness and blindness.

How will John receive new life? He will have to be resurrected, raised from the dead. A few moments ago we saw what Paul said about the natural man being dead in sin. The passage was Ephesians 2:1-3. Now look at how Paul followed it up: 'But because of his great love for us, God, who is rich in mercy, made us alive with Christ even when we were dead in transgressions — it is by grace you have been saved. And God raised us up with Christ and seated us with him in the heavenly realms' (Eph. 2:4-6). In order to save ungodly men, God must raise them from the dead. That is the way the Ephesians were saved. That is the way the apostle Paul was saved. And that is the way that John will be saved, if the Lord is pleased to save him. It will be a work of Christ exercising his kingship, if John is ever saved. Then he will say from the heart, when he sees the lost, 'There, but for the grace of God, go I.' Then he will know what Paul meant in Ephesians 2:8-9: 'For it is by grace you have been saved, through faith — and this not from yourselves, it is the gift of God — not by works, so that no one can boast.'[1]

If a dead man cannot raise himself, and if he does not deserve to be raised, then the work must be *in its entirety* a gracious work of God. *After* a man is raised from the dead, he may do a great deal, but until that moment, he can do nothing. God must do all. As Paul says, 'It does not, therefore, depend on man's desire or effort, but on God's mercy' (Rom. 9:16).

Or take the matter of man's blindness. A blind man, cured by Jesus, once said, 'Nobody has ever heard of opening the eyes of a man born blind' (John 9:32). In healing the physically blind the Lord Jesus did what no other man could do. But spiritual blindness is something much more severe. A man who is physically blind can want to, and ask to, be healed because he knows that he needs his sight; he understands that he is blind. But the blind sinner is totally unaware that he has no understanding of spiritual things. This is how the Reformer, Martin Luther, described him: 'But the Scripture sets before us a man who is not only bound, wretched, captive, sick and dead, but who, through the operation of Satan his lord, adds to his other miseries that of blindness, so that he believes himself to be free, happy, possessed of liberty and ability, whole and alive... Hence, the work of Satan is to hold men so that they do not recognize their wretchedness.'

In writing that way Luther might have been sketching the men Jesus dealt with in John. He offered them freedom if they would hold to his teaching. But they were unable to see what it was that Jesus was saying. 'They answered him, "We are Abraham's descendants and have never been slaves of anyone. How can you say that we shall be set free?"' (John 8:33).

Can men be slaves and not know it? Can they be blind to their own condition? Clearly the answer is, 'Yes'. But what sort of men could be in that awful state? That is a tricky question and we must be careful how we answer it. We are likely to look around us to see if we can find some wretches who have cast off all decency and restraint, and then say, 'Aha! There are the men who are slaves to sin. They had better wake up and realize their bondage!' But that was not the Lord Jesus' view at all. 'I tell you the truth,' he said, 'everyone who sins is a slave to sin' (John 8:34). There is no need to tour heaven and earth to find the slaves Jesus speaks of. We are all such slaves, unless the Son of God has set us free. 'If the Son sets you free, you will be free indeed' (John 8:36) applies to all of us. Christians have never reserved that statement for a special kind of sinner. Either I have been set free by the Lord Jesus, or I am a slave to sin. It is as simple as that.

Long after I had learned to say, 'Yes, I am a sinner,' I had no idea that I had been a slave to sin. If someone had asked me, I would have said that by my 'free will' I could have left my sin and turned to Christ at any time. In other words, I thought of myself as having been free all along. A sinner? Yes, I would have admitted that. But a slave to sin, bound to serve Satan unless the Lord Jesus chose to free me? No, I would have said, I could have escaped at any time.

What would it have taken for me to have escaped? I know the answer now: a new birth. I would have had to have been born again. If God had made me into a different kind of person, given me a new nature, so that I hated sin and saw his glory, then I could have left the old life immediately. But I was dead towards God. To borrow Ezekiel's figure, I had a heart of stone and I needed a heart of flesh (see Ezek. 36:26). God had to give me life and open my eyes before I could see my own sinful state and glimpse his glory and the beauty of Christ. And that is just what he did. It was entirely his work; I had no part in it at all. To him belongs all the praise and glory!

'But,' someone asks, 'didn't you have to make a decision to be born again?' No, I did not. If God had waited for my decision, the act of a man utterly dead towards God, he would still be waiting. Remember, I was blind, I was dead and I hated God, and to top it all,

I didn't know it! For years after I became a Christian I did not realize my former bondage, though it is plainly written in the Word of God. How desperate was my plight as a lost sinner!

After my new birth (and because of it!) I have made many decisions. The new birth had an immediate twofold effect on my will: it moved me to believe in Christ and to seek to avoid sin for his sake. In other words, it brought me to faith and repentance, the very things that are usually meant when Christians speak of 'decisions'. And that was just the beginning. Since then I try to weigh every choice I make in the light of those two great facts. There are plenty of decisions that arise from my being born again, but the new birth itself was God's decision, a decision for which I shall be eternally grateful.

Before I close this chapter let me take up two questions that often come up when we study the new birth. The first one is this: if the new birth is a matter of God's decision, what is the point of preaching the gospel? Will God not save all of his elect anyway? The answer to this question calls for careful thought on our part.

It is clear from Scripture that we must preach the gospel of Christ. If our ideas about how men are saved contradict this command, so much the worse for our ideas! 'Woe to me,' said Paul, 'if I do not preach the gospel!' (1 Cor. 9:16). Paul said this, with his own special commission in view, of course, but, in a measure, we may all say the same thing. We must do good to all men, and the best thing we can do for any man is to tell him about Jesus Christ. We must seek to make him a disciple of our Lord. That has been called 'the Great Commission', and rightly so!

Does this preaching of the gospel have anything to do with the salvation of men? Yes, it does. The connection is quite simple once you see it. In the case of people who are capable of hearing and understanding, God has tied the new birth to the gospel. Men who do not hear or read the gospel are not born again. The new birth takes place among those who learn the good news of Christ. So then, if God has made up his mind to save a man, he has also decided to bring him under the sight or sound of the gospel. The two go hand in hand. As the King of circumstances, God is well able to bring these two things together. In Paul's words, 'Faith comes from hearing the message, and the message is heard through the word of Christ' (Rom. 10:17). If there is no message, there can be no faith. But God provides both for his elect. As a theologian might put it, 'The same

God that ordained the end (the salvation of a particular man), also ordained the means to that end (the hearing of the gospel).'

That brings me to a final question. Does a man have to wait until he is born again to exercise faith? Suppose you, for instance, are not yet a Christian. Must you wait for the new birth to turn from your sins and turn to Christ? What is a man to do who hears the gospel? How should he react? These are burning issues for anyone who thinks deeply about the gospel of Christ.

God commands the man who hears the message of Christ to turn immediately to Christ in faith and repentance. He must wait for nothing. You must wait for nothing, if you are that man!

It is very common to call the new birth an 'experience'. I hear Christians say that they have 'experienced the new birth'. Now there may be nothing wrong in speaking that way. An experience, we may say, is anything that has happened to us. In that sense every believer has experienced the new birth. There are no Christians who have not been born again. However, there are some things that happen to us that we know only indirectly, by their effects, and the new birth is one of those things. The word 'experience', on the other hand, usually carries with it the idea of direct knowledge.

Let me give an example to make clear what I mean. Imagine with me a tasteless pill that would make you twice as strong as you are now. Suppose further that someone mixed it into your food without your knowing it. Would you experience that pill? Not directly. You would not remember crunching it with your teeth or savouring its flavour. You would not even know that you had taken it until you felt its effects. Even then you might not know what you had eaten, but you would know that something unusual had happened to you. You would experience the new strength, the effect of the pill.

The new birth is like that pill. It gives a man or woman the strength and determination to repent and believe. You never experience the new birth apart from its immediate effects, faith and repentance. If I believe in Christ then I know that I have been born again. As I wrote in *Faith: the Gift of God*, 'Apart from repentance and faith I cannot feel or discover the new birth. There is no way to know that I have been born again except by my new attitudes toward God and Christ. Those new attitudes are repentance and faith. If I refuse to turn to Christ until after I feel the new birth I shall never turn. The gospel does not tell me to feel the new birth and then to turn to Christ. It commands me to turn now! And it assures me that when

I do so, I have given all the evidence that I can give that I have been born again.'

If you genuinely want to turn to God through Christ, that is a work of the Spirit of God. So there is no reason to hold back; there is every reason to press forwards in faith and repentance. Do not ask, 'Have I been born again?' Instead, turn from your sin and cast yourself on the mercy of God. The way of peace and safety does not lie in the sinner. It lies in looking on the Lord Jesus in faith. The man who looks to Jesus in faith proves that he has been born again.

Notes

1. In the only other place in the New Testament where the phrase 'not by works' is used, it is clear that absolutely all human activity of any kind is excluded. Paul uses it in Romans 9:12 of God's election of Jacob and rejection of Esau before the twins were born. The phrase translated 'not by works' is identical in Greek as well as English.

10.
God's new kingdom

We have seen that God acts as King in the new birth. Have you come to God and received life? Then the kingship or sovereignty of God brought you to him. In the new birth God works as a moral sovereign. He changed the bias of your life and began to make your motives what they ought to be. And what a change it was! It was like opening the eyes of a blind man, or freeing a captive from slavery, or raising a man from the dead.

But the new birth is just a start. Clearly, there is a big difference between a group of individuals and a people or a nation. God's plan was not simply to save a large number of isolated units, individual men and women, boys and girls. He had made up his mind to have a new humanity, a new society. Nothing less would do.[1] But there could be no new humanity, no new nation, until the coming of 'the kingdom of God'. In the next chapter we will look at the new humanity, but for now let us try to understand the New Testament idea of the kingdom.

Mark introduces it in this way: 'After John was put in prison, Jesus went into Galilee, proclaiming the good news of God. "The time has come," he said. "The kingdom of God is near. Repent and believe the good news!"' (Mark 1:14-15). What did Jesus mean? I suspect that the phrase 'kingdom of God' is a rather vague notion to most of us.

Today the word 'kingdom' suggests a territory, a realm, or the wide expanse of a country and what it contains. That is the meaning we usually give it in modern English and that is sometimes its meaning in the New Testament. When Herod promised the daughter of Herodias whatever she asked, 'up to half my kingdom', he was thinking, no doubt, of the large number of material things under his control. But in the phrase 'the kingdom of God' the word 'kingdom' normally means the 'kingship', 'reign', 'power' or 'sovereignty' of God. Jesus' good news or gospel message was: 'The time has come. The sovereignty of God is virtually upon you. Believe it — and live as if you believe it!' The kingdom of God that Jesus announced was the sovereignty of God.

What I am saying, however, raises an important question. Has God not always reigned, has he not always been sovereign? Of course he has! I would be the last one to deny that — that is, after all, the theme of this book. As the psalmist wrote, 'The Lord has established his throne in heaven, and his kingdom rules over all' (Ps. 103:19). Yes, God has always been King. The reign of God was an old, old truth when Jesus said, 'The sovereignty of God is virtually upon you!' What, then, did he mean?

We can grasp what the Lord meant if we compare his message with other passsages in the New Testament. For instance, John tells us, 'The law was given through Moses; grace and truth came through Jesus Christ' (John 1:17). These words mean that a time came when Jesus Christ brought grace and truth to men.[2] But we all know that there was a great deal of grace and truth in the world before Jesus came. John means that when Jesus came we entered the time of grace abundant, grace without equal, grace shouted from the housetops!

In the same way Paul speaks of 'faith' coming. 'Now that faith has come,' he tells the Galatians, 'we are no longer under the supervision of the law' (Gal. 3:25). Of course, there was 'faith' in Old Testament times — Paul often insists on that — but this is the age characterized by faith, the time to preach faith as never before. So this is the age of the kingdom or sovereignty of God, as it is the age of faith and grace.

That brings us to another question. Perhaps there were relatively less faith and less grace before Jesus came, but can that be said of God's sovereignty? Faith may increase, grace also. But if God has always been sovereign — if he has ruled all things — how can Jesus speak of the coming of God's sovereignty? The answer to that question is what the 'kingdom of God' is all about.

Earlier we saw that there are two things that may be called God's sovereignty.

First there is *God's rule over circumstances and events,* over what happens in this world. Glancing around us we see thousands of events. Each of them happens because God is in control. Not one of them is outside his plan. That has always been true. Over circumstances and events God has reigned completely, in both Old and New Testaments.

But we also saw a second way God rules. I called it *'God's moral sovereignty'*. It has to do, not with *what* happens but, with *why* it happens. Men left to themselves do nothing out of love for God's glory. In that way their motives are wrong. The chief thing, love for God, is never there; it is always missing. Yet what they do remains under God's control. The circumstances and events that they produce are still part of his plan. But people never act from godly motives unless God steps in and changes their hearts. For men's motives to be godly, God must exercise his moral sovereignty. That is a step beyond his simply controlling what happens in this world.

Now we can see in what way the Old Testament looked forward to the sovereignty of God and why Jesus could speak of God's sovereignty as about to appear. Just as faith and grace were to burst abundantly forth with the coming of the Lord Jesus, so God's moral sovereignty would be seen as never before. After all, how does God display his grace? How does he produce faith? By exercising his moral sovereignty. By changing the hearts of men. Did God not do that in Old Testament times? Of course he did! But compared to the earlier age God's work today is astonishing in its reach! In a sense the earth is already filled with the knowledge of the Lord. The gospel has transformed men and women and children — millions of them — in every part of the globe.

But that is not all. If the gospel, or good news, is about God's sovereignty, it also centres in Jesus Christ. Mark makes this plain in the first chapter of his book. The gospel in verses 14-15 is that 'The kingdom [sovereignty] of God is near,' but in verse 1 the gospel is 'about Jesus Christ, the Son of God'. This is no contradiction. Not at all! According to Mark you simply cannot have this new phase of God's kingship without Jesus Christ. The two are tied together. We must never try to pry them apart!

How close is this connection? For one thing, Jesus was the perfect example of a man under the moral sovereignty of God. If we want to know what kind of people this sovereignty of God will finally produce, the Lord Jesus is the answer. In that way, as an example, the Lord Jesus is tightly joined to God's moral sovereignty.

Then again, it was the death of Christ that freed God to exercise his moral sovereignty. If God was to change hearts and to forgive sins he had to do it on a just basis. I do not mean, of course, that anyone was standing over him saying, 'You must act justly!' That could never be! (It is only silly human beings that get the idea that anyone can dictate to God!) No, it was his own character that demanded justice, and he found that justice in the death of his Son. Under the old covenant God looked ahead to Jesus' death for sinners. Now he looks back at it. In both cases God's hands would have been tied by love for his own justice if it had not been for the sacrifice of his Son. Here too Jesus is closely linked to God's new sovereignty.

We have not yet come to the heart of this connection between the Lord Jesus and God's new sovereignty, however. It lies in this startling fact: the Lord Jesus has become the King! When we read of the kingdom or sovereignty of God in the New Testament we are being prepared for a staggering truth. The kingdom, or sovereignty, of God has become the kingdom or sovereignty of Jesus Christ.[3] No wonder Mark tells us that this good news of the kingdom is the story of the Lord Jesus!

Let's take a closer look at this. At the end of his earthly life Jesus said, 'All authority in heaven and on earth has been given to me' (Matt. 28:18). In saying this he meant, 'I am now the King! I have told you that God's sovereignty was coming. It is here, and I am the Sovereign. My Father has made me, the God-man, Lord of both heaven and earth. The whole course of events and circumstances, as well as the changing of hearts, is now under my direction. I am King of kings and Lord of lords!'

I have called this staggering; let me explain why. At first glance it seems as if Father and Son had changed places. Can any rule be wider than 'all authority in heaven and on earth'? Yet that is the claim. It has only one exception. 'It is clear that this does not include God [the Father] himself, who put everything under Christ' (1 Cor. 15:27). All else is under Jesus' sway.

Let me emphasize that both kinds of sovereignty are now in the hands of our Lord Jesus. Listen to him in the first two verses of John 17: 'Father, the time has come. Glorify your Son, that your Son may glorify you. For you granted him authority over all people that he might give eternal life to all those you have given him.' 'Over *all* people' — his authority extends even to those he will not save. What kind of authority can this be? This must be the authority that shapes their circumstances, since it is not his moral sovereignty.[4]

Why does the Lord Jesus need *all* authority to save his own people? The Lord has chosen to save his people by the spread of his Word. He does not do this in a vacuum. Men and women in places where the gospel has never gone are not suddenly 'zapped' by saving power. They must hear God's Word. Without it they remain lost. But here comes the main point: as long as Christ has chosen earthly means for bringing men to himself, he must control all that happens in this world. Not only must missionaries go forth, but people must be raised and trained to fly the planes and run the trains and navigate the rivers to the places where his elect are hidden. Others must produce the tools to reach them, things like loudspeakers and radios. Still others must invent and develop these tools and all else that makes life possible for pioneering men. The progress of material culture in this world is not an accident. It is the work of the God-man, Jesus Christ! We do not have to ask, 'Who is sufficient for these things?' We know the answer: his sovereignty is well able to accomplish all his will.

Let me make this more personal. Take your own conversion if you are a believer in Christ. How could he be sure that you would hear the gospel? He couldn't leave it to chance, could he? No, in order to be sure, he had to arrange your circumstances and the affairs of the man or woman who carried the gospel to you. And what was true of you was true of all other believers — millions of them.

Nor is that all! There was the power of Satan and his armies to be dealt with. Satan had blinded your mind against the truth of God and the attractiveness of Christ. It was not enough that you heard the gospel. Christ had to break the spell of the devil on your life.

If you are a believer in Christ you are a new person with new attitudes and goals and loves and hatreds. Someone had to create those things in you. That 'someone' was the Holy Spirit. But who sent the Spirit? The Lord Jesus! You see, then, how Christ had to control both heaven and earth for even one sinner like yourself to be saved. And he has saved not just one sinner, but millions!

Can we deny him the name of 'King' in the fullest, richest sense? We cannot and we will not! All authority is his, both in heaven and on earth. His kingship is the promised 'kingdom of God'.

Notes

1. 'The important thing to emphasize is that the biblical hope is not one of spiritual salvation alone, of the salvation of the individual from his guilt and his sin... The primary emphasis is upon the salvation of the people of God as a society dwelling on the earth and their deliverance from all evils — spiritual, social, political, and physical' (G. E. Ladd, *A Commentary on the Revelation of John,* Eerdmans, 1972, p. 84). He cites Isaiah 11:9-10 as evidence.

2. Some have thought that John means that all grace and truth in the world *at any time* came through Christ. That may be true, but it is not John's point. His statement is historical, not timeless. He means that at a given time in the history of fallen man, centuries after the Fall, Jesus Christ appeared, bringing grace and truth. It happened, in fact, at the very time John was living.

3. This does not mean that God the Father is no longer King. Keep in mind that the Lord Jesus does his Father's will and that there is a real sense in which what we do through our agents is done by ourselves. Christ is his Father's agent.

4. The phrase 'all people' is literally 'all flesh'. It is commonly used in the Old Testament to mean all men *without exception* (Num. 16:22; Isa. 40:5-6; Jer. 32:27). That is the meaning I am assuming here. In Acts 2:17 where Peter quotes Joel 2:28 (3:1 in the Hebrew), it is used to mean all kinds of men, all men *without distinction*.

11.
God's new humanity

We come out into daylight when we learn that Jesus Christ is now King. But what will he do with his kingship? That is the question. Will he simply do what God has done in the past? If so, what would be new, beyond a shift in activity from Father to Son? Will he simply save men, as God has saved men throughout the Old Testament? No, he will do more than that. He will form those whom he saves into a new body, a new society, a new humanity. We shall be more than new men with a new King. We shall be a new nation that will last for ever.

First, let's take a look back. In the Old Testament God formed a people for himself, the nation of Israel. That was quite a work! Moses expresses something of the wonder of it: 'Has any god ever tried to take for himself one nation out of another nation, by testings, by miraculous signs and wonders, by war, by a mighty hand and an outstretched arm, or by great and awesome deeds, like all the things the Lord your God did for you in Egypt before your very eyes?' (Deut. 4:34). No. No god had ever done a thing like that. God formed Israel by a great display of his power.

However, Israel was not God's new humanity. Her history shows that too clearly. God's kingship in making and keeping the nation together was his control of events and circumstances much more than his moral kingship. We see this from the start, don't we? The sea was hardly behind them when Israel began to complain. They grumbled against the Lord. God's power changed their circumstances but, in the case of most, not their hearts.

Some Israelites, of course, had new hearts from God. But neither were they God's new humanity. They remained a part of the older people of God, the nation of Israel. The new people of God, the new nation, had not yet been formed in Old Testament times. God asserted his moral kingship over some men and women within Israel, but they remained a part of the old nation.[1]

All that was to change with the coming of the Lord Jesus. The church that is his body was about to be formed when Christ began his public ministry. Now, 2,000 years later, we who belong to Christ rejoice to be part of that same body. Let's see how it came into being.

The work of Christ is tied up with the 'new covenant'. The writer of Hebrews looks back into the Old Testament and finds there a promise of a new covenant unlike the one that God made with Israel:

'The time is coming, declares the Lord,
    when I will make a new covenant
with the house of Israel
    and with the house of Judah.
It will not be like the covenant
    I made with their forefathers
when I took them by the hand
    to lead them out of Egypt,
because they did not remain faithful to my covenant,
    and I turned away from them,
                                          declares the Lord.
This is the covenant I will make with the house of Israel
    after that time, declares the Lord.
I will put my laws in their minds,
    and write them on their hearts.
I will be their God,
    and they will be my people.
No longer will a man teach his neighbour,
    or a man his brother, saying, "Know the Lord,"
because they will all know me,
    from the least of them to the greatest.
For I will forgive their wickedness
    and will remember their sins no more'
                        (Heb. 8:8-12, quoting Jer. 31:31-34).

A few telling points are made here. First, the new covenant *was still future* when God gave it through Jeremiah. 'The time is coming,' God said. Again we read, 'after that time'. The new covenant was not operating in Old Testament times. Second, unlike the old covenant, the new covenant would be *unbreakable*. Third, the reason it would be unbreakable is that '*They will all know [the Lord]*, from the least of them to the greatest.' Those who know the Lord do not break his covenants. Fourth, the new covenant concerns *an entire nation* and not just individuals.

It is this last point that I need to dwell on. The people that Jeremiah describes as having God's laws 'on their hearts' are people who have been born again. But the new birth, or something very much like it, must also have existed under the Old Testament. No one could be saved and serve God rightly unless God gave him or her a new heart. Men's hearts have always been 'deceitful above all things and beyond cure' (Jer. 17:9). So when God saved the first man he must have given him a new heart.

What, then, is new about the 'new covenant'? One distinctive feature of the new covenant is that God is forming *a nation* of people who have all been born again — every one of them! We call that new nation the church. Israel, as that name was used 2,000 times in the Old Testament, was largely an unregenerate nation. Their hearts were stubborn. They broke God's laws repeatedly and they did not repent. Yet Israel was God's people and God was their God. He was not simply the God of the godly part of the nation. More than 100 times in the Old Testament God speaks of 'my people', and in dozens of those cases he is lamenting their sins! The nation of Israel was his people, but it was often ungodly.

It was God's plan to form a *godly* nation. That is what the new covenant is about. I have called that nation the church, but Jeremiah calls it 'the house of Israel'. We can see three reasons for this.

First, *the earliest Christians were all Israelites*. The twelve apostles were all Jews. If you had been watching the work of God on the Day of Pentecost you would have seen Israelites — 3,000 of them — pouring into the Christian church. You could have said, 'There is Israel indeed!' The new covenant was first fulfilled in Israel alone, so that the whole church, the whole new nation, was Jewish. Since we who live today see a largely Gentile church in our world, we are likely to forget what it was like at first.

Second, *God has promised that a day will come when the great mass of Israelites will be converted to Christ*. That seems to me to be the most obvious way to understand Paul in the following passage: 'As far as the gospel is concerned, they are enemies on your account; but as far as election is concerned, they are loved on account of the patriarchs, for God's gifts and his call are irrevocable' (Rom. 11:28-29). God will yet call Israel to himself.

Third, *it has pleased God to give the church many names and privileges that were earlier offered to Israel* (see, e.g., 1 Peter 2:9-10). This shows, I think, that God wants us to think of the church as the new Israel. His new covenant really is made with Israel, this new Israel that will include a great mass from the old nation of Israel as well. That is why Paul thinks of the church as the fulfilment of promises made to Israel. He writes to the Romans about the church as God's people whom he has 'called, not only from the Jews but also from the Gentiles' (Rom. 9:24). To clinch his point Paul quotes an Old Testament promise to Israel:

'I will call them "my people" who are not my people;
   and I will call her "my loved one"
who is not my loved one'

(Rom. 9:25, quoting Hosea 2:23).

He sees this promise to Israel fulfilled in the church.

How can Paul take a prediction that refers to Israel and apply it to the church? Paul, I think, would answer us like this: the great promises to Israel are for the Messiah's (Christ's) community, and God planned that community to be made up of Jews. But it would not stop there. It would reach beyond Jews to others. When God gave that promise to Hosea he had the Messianic community in view, the society we call 'the church', or 'the body of Christ'. [2]

But what do we mean by 'the body of Christ'? First, we need to keep in mind that 'the body of Christ' is a figure of speech. It is no use trying to imagine God's people as some sort of creature that looks like a human body. Not at all! It is true that in more than one place Paul compares the church to a human body. He writes, for instance, 'The body is a unit, though it is made up of many parts; and though all its parts are many, they form one body. So it is with Christ' (1 Cor. 12:12). His point is plain: the church, like my body and yours, is a unit that contains various kinds of members — what is called 'unity in diversity'. In the next verses Paul makes that point repeatedly. We need one another, he says. We cannot do without one another; but we do not need each member to be like every other member in every way. The human body is a clear illustration of these simple facts!

Sometimes when Paul speaks of Christ as the 'Head' of the body he has probably added to the figure of the human body (cf. 1 Cor. 11:3). 'Head' in this case means the kind of thing we mean when we say, 'George is the head of a great corporation.' The church is a body of men and women and children with Jesus Christ as its chief. A human head with its flesh and bone is not what he has in mind here. The idea is rather of a society with its leader. Christ is head over the church, just as he is 'head over everything' (Eph. 1:22), 'the Head over every power and authority' (Col. 2:10). He is King.

But if it is true that Christ is King over all that exists, it is true too that the church has a special place in his heart and in his plans. The church is his body (of men and women) in a way that nothing else is or can be. He loved the church before he formed the worlds. Today he rules these same worlds for her sake: 'God placed all things under his feet and appointed him to be head over everything for the church, which is his body' (Eph. 1:22-23).

How close is this bond between Christ and his body? Very close indeed! The Bible speaks of two kinds of union between the Lord Jesus and his people.

First, there is *representative* union. Christ represented us in dying in the sense that he took our place. When he died we died. By 'we' I mean all of God's elect from all ages. That does not mean that in some mysterious way we were literally present at the cross. It means that he acted for us, even before we existed except in the mind of God. What he did is like what the founders of my country did when they signed the Declaration of Independence from Great Britain. Acting for me, they determined that I would be an American citizen even though I was not yet born. They did not think of my name or my person when they wrote their signatures because they were not gods but mere men. But the Lord Jesus knew me even at the cross. He knew you also if you are one of his people. He represented us both in dying.

That is why Paul can speak of the Lord as the one 'who loved *me* and gave himself for *me*' (Gal. 2:20). Notice the personal note in Paul's words. Jesus had Paul in mind when he died. He represented Paul at the cross. Christ did not represent all men in his death. As Paul says elsewhere, 'Christ loved the church and gave himself up for her' (Eph. 5:25). He represented his people in dying.

Second, the Lord Jesus has a *living,* or *vital,* union with his people. What is a living union? Here, I am afraid, language breaks down. We can hardly tell what a living union is because we do not know what life is. But we recognize life by its effects. If we look at a man and ask whether he has life, we answer by seeing whether he breathes and moves and eats and drinks. If he does those things he is alive!

The evidence of life is growth. I am not thinking here of the growth of individual Christians alone, but of the body of Christ as a unit. Paul describes this growth to the Ephesians: 'From [Christ] the whole body, joined and held together by every supporting ligament, grows and builds itself up in love, as each part does its work' (Eph. 4:16). The presence of Christ gives the church life. This life produces growth.

But there is more here than bare growth. Growth can be a random process, at least as we see it. Take a vine, for example. Watch it grow! What can we say about it? God may have a plan for its expansion and direction, but we cannot tell what that is.

That is not how Paul saw the church, however. Look again at the verse above. Paul saw growth and more. He saw progress as well, in much the same way as a human body moves towards maturity. Jesus Christ is the source of that progress. He is alive in the church and the church is alive in him. If this sounds a bit mystical we must not be put off by it. It is another way of saying that the closest bond possible exists between Christ and his church.

This union between Christ and his people is so close that Paul can startle us by calling Christ and his people simply 'Christ'. Here are his words: 'The body is a unit, though it is made up of many parts; and though all its parts are many, they form one body. So it is with Christ' (1 Cor. 12:12)

Paul learned this fact moments before his own conversion to Christ, when the Lord said to him, '"Saul, Saul, why do you persecute me?" "Who are you, Lord?" Saul asked. "I am Jesus, whom you are persecuting," he replied' (Acts 9:4-5). To persecute the people of Jesus was to persecute Jesus himself. Their pain was his pain; their suffering, his suffering. Can you imagine a closer bond than that?

But let's return to our subject, the kingship of Christ. In fact, we have not left it at all. When Jesus said, 'All authority in heaven and on earth has been given to me,' he already had his eye on forming the church. He sent his disciples to preach and to teach, but their words had no power in themselves. The new birth was Christ's work, by his Spirit. The church was also his work, a work of sovereign power.

That explains something that comes up time and again in the New Testament. We read of someone being saved and in the context there is a mention of God's original act of creation. Or we read of Christ and the church and we find the same thing. No one can think of an event that was more a work of kingship than the creation of heaven and earth. In a burst of sovereignty God made the worlds!

'For by [the Son] all things were created ... all things were created by him and for him. He is before all things, and in him all things hold together. And he is the head of the body, the church' (Col. 1:16-18) There is the comparison. Paul lays the first creation beside the church.

Elsewhere he writes, 'If anyone is in Christ, he is a new creation; the old has gone, the new has come!' (2 Cor. 5:17). There are two creations, then, the old and the new ; and the Son of God, whom we now know as Jesus Christ, is the author of both. The new world that is to come when Jesus Christ returns is already here in part.[3] The new humanity, the church of Jesus Christ, is the down payment on something vaster and more glorious than anything we have yet seen, 'a new heaven and a new earth, the home of righteousness' (2 Peter 3:13).

Notes

1. For a discussion of the relation of saved Israelites under the old covenant to the church see Appendix I.
2. 'This cannot be labelled a manipulation or misuse of the Old Testament; rather, it illustrates something essential in Paul's thought; that Jesus, even though crucified, is the Messiah foretold in the Old Testament, and that the people of the Messiah are the true people of God' (G. E. Ladd, *A Theology Of The New Testament,* Eerdmans, 1974, p. 395).
3. This is much clearer still, if we adopt the translation of the New English Bible: 'When anyone is united to Christ, there is a new world; the old order has gone, and a new order has already begun.'

12.
Preparing for God's new world

We have already seen how Adam's sin set things in this world on their heads in three ways:

1. God was no longer King in a moral sense.
2. Man no longer held the earth in trust for God.
3. Man and the world around him were in disharmony.

This left creation in need of a new humanity, a new earth and a new bond between them. These were drastic reversals, but God knew what he would do. He is never surprised by the deeds of men or of angels. Quite the contrary! He uses all things, including sin, to further his own good and wise purposes. That is part of what we ought to mean when we call him God.

After Adam and Eve sinned there was no man or woman on earth under the moral kingship of God — not even one. So far as man could see, God was robbed of his sovereignty. No doubt Adam and Eve were too occupied with themselves to give much thought to God and his rights. If the question of 'rights' entered their minds at all, they must have thought of God's right to judge their rebellion and bring the promised death on them. His right to rule their hearts — to act as moral Sovereign — was the last thing they would care anything about. If it had come into their heads to think of such things at all, they would probably have excused themselves in the same way we do today by saying, 'We've got our own problems to worry about.' But man's sin was the signal for God to act.

First, here and there, God reasserted his moral kingship by

changing the hearts of his rebels. It seems likely that he started with
Adam and Eve. Stripping them of the leaves they used to hide their
nakedness and clothing them with the skins of slain beasts has often
been thought to picture their salvation. In any case we do know that
early in man's history God was gracious to many, including their
first son, Abel. As time went on God enlarged his activity. When
Christ came there was a leap forward in the extent of the work of
redemption. Today literally millions upon millions of men, women
and children are under the moral kingship of God. Christ is moral
Sovereign over many in the far ends of the earth.

But what of the other two difficulties? Does man again hold the
earth in trust for God? Has the disharmony between man and his
world passed away?

The answer to the first question must be 'Yes and no!' When God
saves a man he destroys that man's self-centredness, not perfectly,
but generally. One effect of God's work is this: the new Christian
discovers that he owns nothing. God owns it all. The Christian is a
steward, a manager, who works for another, God himself. Because
the believer is not perfect he does not carry out his stewardship as
well as he ought to. But to a large degree he now holds what he has
as a trust for God. The Christian uses the earth and its store of
material goods for God's glory once more.

I wish that were the whole story, but it is not. I must add three
more reasons why we cannot return a simple 'Yes' to the question,
'Does man again hold the earth in trust for God?'

First, vast numbers of men are not Christians. These men keep on
in their old ways, not treating the created world as the property of God.

Second, I have already mentioned our own sinfulness, the fact
that Christians are not perfect. Our good intentions are often
frustrated by our poor performance. And — what is worse — our
intentions, our motives are not always right to begin with. These two
facts defeat us.

The third problem is this: there are great powers ranged against
us even when our motives are good ones. Often we are powerless
against these forces. There are things are built into the world as we
know it that will undo our best plans.

That brings us to the other question, has the disharmony between
man and his world passed away? The answer is, no it has not.

Part of the curse on Adam's sin was the curse on the ground. Here
it is:

'Cursed is the ground because of you;
   through painful toil you will eat of it
   all the days of your life.
It will produce thorns and thistles for you,
   and you will eat the plants of the field.
By the sweat of your brow
   you will eat your food'

(Gen. 3:17-19).

There is reluctance on the part of the earth to give up its fruits to man. Ask any farmer! The curse is not the fact that he must work. No, work is a gift from God. Men were made to work and cannot be happy without it. The curse is that the farmer has a fight on his hands. He toils under a relentless sun. He competes with weeds and briars. He watches helplessly while flood and drought destroy his crops. Or else, he beats off all of these evils, only to have his fruits fall prey to voracious insects and marauding animals. It is well written: 'By the sweat of your brow...'!

The curse is given in terms of farming, because agriculture is basic to all life. But we must not be misled by that fact. The curse applies to all labour, mental as well as physical. I started to say all legitimate labour, but I am not so sure that I must limit it in that way. It is true that some men live off the toil of others, but even they have to engage in a good deal of taxing mental stress to survive. Exhaustion — mental, physical or emotional — is the common lot of men in this fallen world. God in his sovereignty has seen to that.

Not only that, but the world lives under another, even more painful curse. I am thinking of the tireless activity of Satan and his demon armies.

You may remember the temptation of Christ, the one in which Satan offered to give the Lord Jesus all the kingdoms of the world, with their authority and splendour. 'It has been given to me,' Satan said, 'and I can give it to anyone I want to. So if you worship me, it will all be yours' (Luke 4:6). The devil is a liar, of course, and we dare not always believe him. He is an usurper. Whatever he has, he has stolen. Yet that is not the whole story. The Bible recognizes that this world is in Satan's hands in some sense. 'The whole world,' John wrote, 'is under the control of the evil one' (1 John 5:19). The Lord Jesus called him 'the prince of this world' (John 14:30).

Is it any wonder that Paul says the whole creation groans 'as in the pains of childbirth right up to the present time'? (Rom. 8:22). What else could it do?

One phrase, however, in Paul's lament deserves a second look because it holds out hope. He speaks of 'the pains of childbirth'. Now we know that the pains of childbirth are a special kind of pain. They are not pointless, as so many of our pains seem to us to be. They remind the mother-to-be that she is about to have her child. They are the promise of great joy to come.

When the creation groans, it groans in hope 'that the creation itself will be liberated from its bondage to decay and brought into the glorious freedom of the children of God' (Rom. 8:21). That is very important. It points up the need for a new world and more. The groans of this world look forward to the promise of a better world to come.

How shall such a new world come? It will come through the kingship, the sovereignty, of Jesus Christ. In the rest of this chapter I hope to show how the Lord Jesus has already been exerting his kingship to bring about this new world. In the next chapter we shall look at that world itself.

Once when Jesus drove out a demon the Pharisees accused him of being in league with the devil. He responded in this way: 'Any kingdom divided against itself will be ruined, and a house divided against itself will fall. If Satan is divided against himself, how can his kingdom stand? ... But if I drive out demons by the finger of God, then the kingdom of God has come to you. When a strong man, fully armed, guards his own house, his possessions are safe. But when someone stronger attacks and overpowers him, he takes away the armour in which the man trusted and divides up the spoils' (Luke 11:17-18,20-22).

Here is the Lord's own view of what he would first have to do to form his new heavens and earth. He saw that Satan has sovereignty that stands opposed to the kingship of God, and he saw himself in a death struggle to strip Satan of his powers so that he might carry out his plans.

Jesus began this stripping of Satan in his public ministry. He was the one who took away the strong man's goods. When he freed men from demons he was taking them from Satan. In that one act Satan, the Pharisees and all other men could see that the King-designate had come among them.

At the same time, the casting out of demons and the other

miracles served a larger purpose. They blessed the men whom Jesus helped, of course, but they did more. They were typical acts as well, acts that looked ahead to greater things. When the Lord set men free from demons and illness, he was picturing the future destruction of Satan and of all the evils that prey on men in this world. He was also anticipating the day when he would ascend to the Father, sit down at his right hand, and become King of kings and Lord of lords.

The main attack on the devil's kingship came at the cross. That was already dimly foreseen in the Old Testament when God promised Eve a child who would bruise Satan's head while receiving a wound of his own (Gen. 3:15). The Lord Jesus was that child and it was at the cross that he felt the devil's blow. On the Mount of Olives he said to the men who were Satan's tools, 'This is your hour — when darkness reigns' (Luke 22:53). He put himself into their hands and in less than twenty-four hours they had done their worst. They nailed him to the cross.

But here Satan overplayed his hand. The death of Christ was the plan of God, a plan that expressed God's wisdom. Satan and his associates, both human and demonic, did not grasp what God was doing. 'None of the rulers of this age understood [God's wisdom], for if they had, they would not have crucified the Lord of glory' (1 Cor. 2:8). Why not? Not because they were too nice to do so — not at all! The reason was this: the cross was the beginning of their own undoing and they did not know it! There is a sense, then, in which Jesus may be said to have already reigned on the cross. The human powers that crucified the Lord Jesus were ignorant of God's plan, but so too were the demonic hosts that drove them on, including Satan himself.

Jesus knew that the devil's destruction was tied up with his death. With his eye on the cross he said, 'Now the prince of this world will be driven out' (John 12:31). Years later, in writing to the Colossian Christians, Paul made the same point to them. They were in danger of thinking too highly of spiritual forces ('thrones or powers or rulers or authorities' — Col. 1:16). Christ, Paul wrote, 'is the head over every power and authority' (Col. 2:10). How could that be? God used the cross to bring them under. 'And having disarmed the powers and authorities, he made a public spectacle of them, triumphing over them by the cross' (Col. 2:15).

The writer to the Hebrews makes the same point more fully: 'Since the children have flesh and blood, [Christ] too shared in their humanity so that by his death he might destroy him who holds the

power of death — that is, the devil' (Heb. 2:14). The death of Christ
was Satan's death as well!

That brings me to one last point. Is Satan really destroyed? Not
long ago we heard that 'Satan is alive and well on planet earth!'
Which is it?

If you read much academic theology, you will have come across
a recurring phrase, 'already — not yet!' Those three words light up
more than one scriptural truth. Here are some examples.

Are Christians saved? Yes or no? I think we would all answer
'Yes' to that question. We might quote Ephesians 2:8, where Paul
tells the Ephesian Christians, 'It is by grace you have been saved.'
Yes, we are already saved! But sometimes the Scripture speaks of
our salvation as yet future. When I was young I heard a preacher end
his prayer with the words: 'And save us at last for Jesus' sake.' In
my ignorance I smiled a superior smile at that prayer, but I was
wrong to do so. 'Watch your life and doctrine closely,' Paul wrote
to Timothy. 'Persevere in them, because if you do, you will save
both yourself and your hearers' (1 Tim. 4:16). Was Timothy saved?
Not yet! Salvation is a broad term that includes a good deal that is
not yet done in us. We are saved already, but not yet!

We can ask the same kind of question about our adoption into
God's family. Have we been adopted or not? Paul treated our
adoption as a fact in Galatians 4:5-6. We have the full rights of sons
— already! But in Romans 8:23 he wrote, 'We wait eagerly for our
adoption as sons.' So there is a sense in which it is not yet!

Suppose we ask if we have been glorified yet? We would answer
that with a resounding no, wouldn't we? Not yet! But Paul writes,
'Those [God] justified, he also glorified' (Rom. 8:30). Does he
mean this has already happened?

How can we explain these odd statements? They should not
cause us too much difficulty if we keep in mind one fact: all through
history there have been decisive events, events that determined a
great deal that came later. In a war, for example, we hear of a
decisive battle. Someone says, 'The war was over after that battle.'
What does he mean? Doesn't he know that combat went on for
months longer? Yes, he knows that, but, in a sense, it made no
difference to the outcome, though it may have made a good deal of
difference to those who continued fighting. Some of them were
wounded and some died. But still it was true that the war was won
and lost long before.

Sometimes a word or two from a powerful man can be decisive.

Ancient courtiers used to say, 'It is done, Your Majesty!' How could they say such a thing when they knew they had not yet started to carry out his orders? Were they lying? Not at all! What they meant was that the king's word was decisive. His command would be carried out; his will would be done.

Let's come back to Satan and his destruction. Was he destroyed by the death of Christ? Yes, he was. In what sense? In several senses.

First, *his destruction,* like our salvation, *is a process.* Already in the ministry of Jesus his influence over many people was destroyed. For centuries Satan had his way over men throughout the earth. The ministry of Jesus was the signal that such widespread sway was at an end. Jesus Christ would be King.

Second, *the cross was a decisive event in Satan's life.* Without the cross he might have gone on terrorizing men for ever. The death of Christ was the just basis on which God always carried on his work of delivering men from Satan's hands. In Old Testament times God saved men from Satan's clutches in anticipation of the cross. Now he looks back at the completed atonement. In both cases it is the cross that allows him to redeem men righteously. The cross is the devil's undoing.

Finally, *the Lord Jesus has spoken a decisive kingly word against Satan:* 'The prince of this world now stands condemned' (John 16:11). Satan's destruction is as good as done. His judgement is as sure as the word of the King.

What does all of this mean? It means that there will be a new creation, a new heavens and a new earth. It means that God will have a people to populate that new world. And it means that nothing will disturb the peace of that land for ever. The King's word will stand!

We must not, of course, use these facts to excuse us from keeping up the fight. We are like the soldiers who wage war after the decisive battle has been won. If it is already true that Christ has triumphed over every power and authority, it is also true that the war goes on. Paul urged the Ephesians to be fully armed against the devil: 'For our struggle is not against flesh and blood, but against the rulers, against the authorities, against the powers of this dark world and against the spiritual forces of evil in the heavenly realms' (Eph. 6:12)

We have *not yet* come to the new earth where all is peace, but that day is so certain that *already,* 'Everyone born of God overcomes the world. This is the victory that has overcome the world, even our faith. Who is it that overcomes the world? Only he who believes that Jesus is the Son of God' (1 John 5:4-5).

13.
The new earth

Let me ask a question. When we pray, 'Thy kingdom come' (Matt. 6:10, AV), what is it that we want from God? The answer, I think, is found in looking at all of verse 10:

'Your kingdom come,
your will be done on earth
    as it is in heaven.'

How is God's will done among his elect angels in heaven? I hope the following words will suggest at least part of the answer. In heaven the will of God is done:

immediately — without sinful delay;
cheerfully — without half-heartedness;
constantly — without interruption;
vigorously — without weariness and exhaustion.

If you take the time you can no doubt add to this list.

When you and I look around us we are tempted to ask if these same words could ever be applied to God's will as it is done on earth. The answer is in this saying of Jesus: 'With man this is impossible, but with God all things are possible' (Matt. 19:26). When we pray for God's will to be done on earth we are asking for his intervention in history. We are asking God to assert himself, to show that he is King.

All through this book we have been looking at God's kingship.

The fact is, God has always been King and this world is a part of his kingdom. The kingdom, or sovereignty, or kingship of God should never be in dispute among Christians. Every circumstance and event that happens in this world serves God's good and wise purposes.

We have also seen that both men and angels have rebelled against God. It is true that what they do furthers God's aims. But there is another pointed truth: fallen men and fallen angels never do what they do for the highest and best reason, so that God will be glorified. We found that in the motives of men God has a vast area in which he may assert another kind of sovereignty, what I have called moral sovereignty or moral kingship. He may work in men's lives to change the bias of their hearts so that they will come to find joy in doing what he commands.

To some extent God has always exercised moral kingship. From the time of the fall of man he gave some men new hearts. But when Christ came the amount of God's saving activity increased so greatly that it seemed as if he had never before been King. Take Pentecost, as an example. On that day multitudes were born again. 3,000 men and women came under God's moral sovereignty at once. Nor was that the end; it was just the beginning! The book of Acts adds to that group time after time until men and women from as far away as Rome itself have been saved in large numbers. And beyond that the church has grown by Christ's sovereign action from that day till this!

Some day this process must end. When the last of God's elect people has been saved the time will have come for judgement and a new world. The one will prepare for the other.[1]

We need to take a closer look at this matter of judgement at the end of the age. The purpose of judgement is to consign men and angels to their respective destinies. I will have more to say about angels in a moment, but let's start with men. The judgement of men and women is pictured in the story of the sheep and the goats in Matthew 25: 'When the Son of Man comes in his glory, and all the angels with him, he will sit on his throne in heavenly glory. All the nations will be gathered before him, and he will separate the people one from another as a shepherd separates the sheep from the goats. He will put the sheep on his right and the goats on his left' (Matt. 25:31-33). Let me point out two facts from the opening of this parable.

First, *judgement is the act of a King*. You will see that we have not left the subject of Christ's kingship; it is the Lord Jesus who is seen here, seated on a glorious throne.

It is also an act of power. The King will physically separate saved men and lost men for ever. We do not know what kind of power he will use, perhaps the force of his spoken word, but whatever power it is, it will produce a great gulf between men that will never be bridged. Nor will it deal with just a mere handful of men. It will place this gulf between the men of all nations. Sovereign power of this kind, considering the billions of people involved, staggers the mind.

Where will these men and women go? 'Then the King will say to those on his right, "Come, you who are blessed by my Father; take your inheritance, the kingdom prepared for you since the creation of the world..." Then he will say to those on his left, "Depart from me, you who are cursed, into the eternal fire prepared for the devil and his angels ..." Then they will go away to eternal punishment, but the righteous to eternal life' (Matt. 25:34,41,46).

The sheep will be blessed for ever, an act of grace from the King. The goats will be cursed for ever, an act of justice. The word of the King is final. And by casting the goats away from his people and his new earth for ever, Christ will have moral kingship over all the people of the earth.

Put another way, this means that Satan will no longer have any subjects. The devil (the 'strong man' of Luke 11:21) will have been stripped of his hold on men, by the work of Christ. He too will be banished, as we see above, 'into eternal fire prepared for [him] and his angels'. Christ's moral kingship will extend over the whole earth then, including all the angels that are left to visit the earth. 'The kingdom of the world has become the kingdom of our Lord and of his Christ, and he will reign for ever and ever' (Rev. 11:15). Never again, through all eternity, will any person, man or angel, disturb the rule of the King of kings.

That brings us to the relation of man to the new earth. We have seen that man and the rest of creation were out of joint in two ways.

First, man was supposed to be holding the earth as a stewardship from God. We know that he failed in that task, and we saw the reasons for his failure. The presence of men who were not under the moral kingship of Christ was one problem. They would not hold the world in trust for God; they wanted it for themselves. Even that was not granted to them; in fact, they were under bondage to Satan and so often used it for his purposes without knowing it. But all of that will be at an end in the new earth. Evil men will be gone, and good men will be perfected so that they will act as God's managers once more.

The second problem with man and the earth was the disharmony that came as a result of sin. That too will be put right. All the curses that fell on man when he sinned will be lifted from his shoulders. There will be perfect harmony between the earth and the man. The phrase 'the right man in the right place' will fit their relationship exactly.

All of this will be the work of the Lord Jesus acting as King. The writer to the Hebrews looked towards the new heaven and earth from the perspective of his day. He saw the Lord Jesus as the one who would make good, in himself and in his people, the plan of God for creation: 'It is not to angels that [God] has subjected the world to come, about which we are speaking. But there is a place where someone has testified:

"What is man that you are mindful of him,
    the son of man that you care for him?
You made him a little lower than the angels;
    you crowned him with glory and honour
    and put everything under his feet."

'In putting everything under him, God left nothing that is not subject to him. Yet at present we do not see everything subject to him. But we see Jesus, who was made a little lower than the angels, now crowned with glory and honour because he suffered death, so that by the grace of God he might taste death for everyone.

'In bringing many sons to glory, it was fitting that God, for whom and through whom everything exists, should make the author of their salvation perfect through suffering' (Heb. 2:5-11).

Here is God's programme in a nutshell. Man was made to rule the world, but we do not see him doing so. What hope is there of his ever ruling all things? Jesus Christ is the hope! He is already crowned; he already rules. And he is saving still others, 'bringing many sons to glory'. They too will rule with him. You will rule with him if you belong to the Lord Jesus. All things will be put under man's feet in connection with Christ, and in that way God's plan will be carried out for ever.

What will this new earth be like? Here again we must refer to the kingship of Christ. Remember that he has 'all authority in heaven and on earth' (Matt. 28:18). We have been watching him use his moral sovereignty to change the hearts of lost men. At this point he will exercise his sovereignty over circumstances and events to make a new world fitted to the new men he has made.

Let me illustrate this from the field of atomic energy. Have you heard the phrase 'critical mass'? It refers to the amount of fuel necessary to create a nuclear reaction. The scientist has some fuel; he adds some more fuel and then some more again. At some point a terrific explosion takes place. He has reached the critical mass.

The Lord Jesus has been adding men and women and children to his church, one at a time or in great numbers. One day he will reach the critical mass. All of his elect will be brought in, and then he will destroy this world and with kingly power he will create a new one. Peter describes what Christ will do in words that remind us of an atomic blast: 'That day will bring about the destruction of the heavens by fire, and the elements will melt in the heat. But in keeping with his promise we are looking forward to a new heaven and a new earth, the home of righteousness' (2 Peter 3:12-13) At last there will be a new humanity, a new earth and a new bond between them.

What kind of world is a new world? Here is John's answer from the book of Revelation: 'Then I saw a new heaven and a new earth, for the first heaven and the first earth had passed away, and there was no longer any sea. I saw the Holy City, the new Jerusalem, coming down out of heaven from God, prepared as a bride beautifully dressed for her husband. And I heard a loud voice from the throne saying, "Now the dwelling of God is with men, and he will live with them. They will be his people, and God himself will be with them and be their God. He will wipe every tear from their eyes. There will be no more death or mourning or crying or pain, for the old order of things has passed away"' (Rev. 21:1-4). Again we read, 'No longer will there be any curse. The throne of God and of the Lamb will be in the city, and his servants will serve him. They will see his face, and his name will be on their foreheads. There will be no more night. They will not need the light of a lamp or the light of the sun, for the Lord God will give them light. And they will reign for ever and ever' (Rev. 22:3-5).

This magnificent picture, along with the rest of chapters 21 and 22, is intended to appeal to our imagination as well as to our intellect.

John did not give us the details of our future life on earth. He meant to stir us up to admiration and wonder, and he has done so. I think it is fair to say that John could not tell us much about eternity because we would not be able to take it in. That is why there is so much figurative language in these two chapters.

However, on the negative side he has told us of several things that we must take quite literally: no more tears, or death, or mourning, or crying, or pain. And, considering how often men have had reason to fear it, he adds this: no more night.

Long ago David wrote, 'Delight yourself in the Lord and he will give you the desires of your heart' (Ps. 37:4). At first glance this seems to be a dangerous promise. What strange desires we sometimes find within ourselves! But the first part of the verse — 'Delight yourself in the Lord' — stands guard over misusing this promise. If we find delight in God and Christ we shall more and more want what they want, and that is what we shall have. That will be the meat and drink of eternity.

All through history God has used his sovereignty for the good of his people. Throughout that same history he has repeatedly set before us glimpses of even greater blessings to come. It seems right to add two things about these promises. First, *God's Word can never fail*. In his own time and in his own way, he will bring all that he has said to pass. Secondly, *all that God has promised is found in the Lord Jesus*. In Paul's graphic phrase, 'No matter how many promises God has made, they are "Yes" in Christ' (2 Cor. 1:20). His kingship or sovereignty comes to us mediated through the gracious acts of our Saviour. Let us trust him; let us give glory to God. It is with God — Father, Son and Spirit — that we shall spend and enjoy eternity.

Notes
1. For an interesting discussion of this connection between judgement and the new world as seen in Revelation 5-6, see Appendix II.

Part IV

Living with the sovereignty of God

14.
On reading God's sovereignty

Once the Lord Jesus rebuked some of his critics with these words: 'When evening comes, you say, "It will be fair weather, for the sky is red," and in the morning, "Today it will be stormy, for the sky is red and overcast." You know how to interpret the appearance of the sky, but you cannot interpret the signs of the times' (Matt. 16:2-3). They should have been able to look around and see that God was at work in a special way. The time of the Messiah, the kingdom of God, was virtually on them, and they missed it

In this book I have been stressing the truth that everything we see around us is, in one sense, the work of God. It all brings about his purposes; every detail of life promotes his plans. The thought is staggering, but it is biblical. God 'works out everything in conformity with the purpose of his will' (Eph. 1:11). So far, so good.

But this fact raises a question. Can we learn God's will by reading his providence? Are you and I in the same position as Jesus' critics? Can we watch what is happening around us and find out what we should do next? Christians do not all agree on the answer to these questions, but it seems clear that the answer we each give will have a great deal to do with how we live our lives. This problem cries out for a solution, and it is not simply a puzzle for theologians.

First, we must remember that God has given us a guide for our lives: his Word. We must form the habit of bringing everything else to this standard. If any conclusion that we draw from the circumstances and events around us contradicts God's Word we may be sure that our conclusion is wrong. God does not contradict himself. His providence will never point one way when his Word points another.

I can imagine someone asking a question at this point: 'If God
has left his Word to guide us, why would anyone seek guidance from
any other source? Why would anyone try to read the events around
them to find out what God wants them to do?' I think there are
several reasons.

First, we all like to be certain when we make our choices, and
religion seems to offer the most certainty that we can attain to. In one
form or another, by dreams or horoscopes or by consulting mediums
or religious leaders, most of the world wants to feel that what it does
will be successful.

Second, while the Bible guides us on all kinds of moral issues,
it does not tell us what choice to make when all the choices seem
morally good. It does not tell us in what city we ought to live, the
name of the company that we must work for, or the person we ought
to marry. We wish it did, but obviously it does not. Did I say
'obviously'? I am afraid that is an overstatement. Some Christians
would not agree. They think that if you put your finger down at
random in the Bible, you may find the answer to questions like these.
Should you marry Mary or Martha? Close your eyes and touch a
page of the New Testament with your finger and you may find out!
But a little thought will show you that that is not a fair way to treat
God's Word. We do not like to be quoted out of context; we know
that leads to our meaning being badly distorted. The same is true of
the Scripture. We only use it rightly when we take its words in the
way they were intended by the writers. Any other use is wrong.

To return to our problem: we want certainty; we want to please
God; so how can we know what to choose when we have no direct
word from the Lord? Can we turn to his providence, his arranging
of the affairs of this world, to help us? I am afraid that we shall have
to get into some deep waters and learn a bit of theology to answer
these questions.

For centuries many scholars have seen that at least two things in
the Bible are called 'the will of God'. They have called one of these
things 'God's decretive will'. There is no mystery about that phrase.
It simply means that whatever God decrees or decides to happen is
in some sense his will. The fact that I am sitting here writing is God's
decretive will. He decided that I would do this, and I am doing it. If
he had decided against it I would not be doing it. I would be doing
something else, eating, drinking, shaving, or who knows what? The
same applies to your reading this page just now. You must be

reading it or you would not know what I have written, but why are you reading this page and not putting out the cat (if you have a cat)? God decreed it; that's why. If he had decided otherwise, you would be doing something else. James makes that plain enough: 'Now listen, you who say, "Today or tomorrow we will go to this or that city, spend a year there, carry on business and make money." Why, you do not even know what will happen tomorrow. What is your life? You are a mist that appears for a little while and then vanishes. Instead, you ought to say, "If it is the Lord's will, we will live and do this or that"' (James 4:13-15) 'If it is the Lord's will!' — God has a will that determines what you and I can or cannot do. As I said earlier, theologians called that 'God's decretive will'.

I can treat the other aspect of the will of God much more briefly. The Bible's commands or precepts are called 'God's preceptive will'. Someone may decide to rob a bank or commit a murder. God forbids these things. They are against his will, that is, against his precepts or commands. The person may indeed carry out the crimes, but in this sense he is acting against God's will. These are moral issues and God says 'No!'

So, to sum up, God's decretive will means simply whatever he wills to happen in this world; his preceptive will is what he commands us to do or not to do.

Now here is the point we need to remember. If we are clear on this it will help us to live out our lives for his glory. God's decretive will is his rule for his own activity; his preceptive will is his rule for us. If we grasp that we will save ourselves a great deal of confusion.

One fact that strikes us as we turn through the pages of the Bible is the number of people who knew some portion of God's decretive will and tried to act upon it, only to be wrong in what they did.

Let's start with Abraham. God told him that he would make Abraham the father of many nations. That was God's decision, his decretive will for Abraham. But that very promise led Abraham to do something that he might otherwise not have done. His wife, Sarah, said to him, 'The Lord has kept me from having children. Go, sleep with my maidservant; perhaps I can build a family through her' (Gen. 16:2). Archaeology has shown that Sarah's suggestion to Abraham was a common means for childless couples to get an heir in their culture. We might debate whether it was right or wrong in itself, but we know that it was the wrong way for Abraham and Sarah to look for the fulfilment of God's promise. Even when we know what God has decreed, it is best to leave the means to God himself. He will act rightly.

Abraham may have done what he did because he knew what God had decreed for the future. We sometimes know what God's decretive will for the future is. We know, for example, that he will destroy the wicked some day, but that is no rule for us. We have nothing to do with that at all; God's decree is his rule for his own activity.

But does the way things happen give us rules as to how we ought to act? Can God's decretive will tell us what to do and show us what judgements to make? In a moment we will look in God's Word to find the answer, but I want to anticipate that answer now. Only in rare cases can God's providence, his sovereignty in what happens around us, tell us what we ought to do. For all practical purposes, the answer is 'No'. God's providence is no rule for our actions or our judgements.

The only exception to this rule that I can find is the case where God closes a door that cannot be opened by anything I can do. Shall I marry Mary or Martha? The answer is no, if Mary and Martha have been killed in the crash of an airliner. Even then, the answer might be, 'Go ahead, if you can!' This is the kind of case where you do not have to reflect on the events at all. Your answer is so obvious that it cannot be missed. And that kind of case, I think, is the only kind in which providence, or God's decretive will, can tell you what to do. We simply do not have the wisdom to read the events around us in the way God would know them and act upon them.

What is the most common case in which we try to determine God's will from our circumstances? From years of talking with Christians I think I know the answer: it is the case in which things are not going well or some calamity has struck, and we wonder if it shows that God is upset with us. 'God must be displeased with me,' we say, 'or this would not have happened to me! Perhaps I am harbouring some secret sin that God wants me to root out.'

Well, I think Job could tell us something about that case, don't you? His friends reasoned the same way. They said, 'God is displeased with Job,' and they didn't stop there. They found in Job's circumstances a rule for their action as well as a rule for their judgement about Job. 'We judge that Job is being punished by God,' they said in effect, 'and it is our duty to make that plain to him.'

Now, Job's friends might have been absolutely right in both their judgement and their act. I repeat, they *might have been*. But, in fact, they were totally wrong! There are men and women and children who displease God and who are disciplined and punished by God. That is clear; there can be no question about that. Further, as we have seen earlier in this book, it is God's hand that we all feel when trial and difficulty come. If Job's friends had been content to say, 'This is from God,' they would have been right. Job himself said the same thing, didn't he? 'The Lord gave and the Lord has taken away' (Job 1:21). Those were his very words, and he followed them up by more of the same. When his wife said, 'Curse God and die!' he rebuked her folly with the telling question: 'Shall we accept good from God, and not trouble?' (Job 2:10). Yes, it was God's hand that Job felt, and it is God's hand that you feel too.

Job's friends might have gone a step further, as well. They might have said to Job, 'Perhaps you should consider if you have sinned against God.' Job's calamity did not lay on them any duty to ask that question; it was no rule for their lives and lips, but it would not have been wrong to ask it. Everything that happens to us, whether good or evil, is a call to us to review our lives and to renew our consecration to God. There is nothing wrong about that — there is everything right about it! But no calamity in this world, however severe, can tell us that God is displeased with us. We must learn that, if we learn it at all, from his Word and not from our circumstances.

The book of Hebrews makes this clear in the following passage about the heroes of faith: 'And what more shall I say? I do not have time to tell about Gideon, Barak, Samson, Jephthah, David, Samuel and the prophets, who through faith conquered kingdoms, administered justice, and gained what was promised; who shut the mouths of lions, quenched the fury of the flames, and escaped the edge of the sword; whose weakness was turned to strength; and who became powerful in battle and routed foreign armies. Women received back their dead, raised to life again.'

This is a favourite passage with me, because of something that happens right at this point. I'll talk about it in a moment, but first let's read on: 'Others were tortured and refused to be released, so that they might gain a better resurrection. Some faced jeers and flogging, while still others were chained and put in prison. They were stoned; they were sawn in two; they were put to death by the sword. They went about in sheepskins and goatskins, destitute, persecuted and ill-treated — the world was not worthy of them. They wandered in deserts and mountains, in caves and holes in the ground' (Heb. 11:32-38). What an account of the faithful people of God!

Imagine how distorted our picture of God's saints would be if we had nothing but the first part of this passage to judge them by. What would we conclude? Just this: that no calamities ever overtook the people of God! Were they engaged in physical warfare? Never mind — they conquered kingdoms! Did they face wild beasts? No matter — they shut the mouths of lions! Were they thrown into fiery furnaces? Fear not — they quenched the fury of the flames! Would anyone blame you if you thought that disaster proved that you were not a child of God or that you had sorely displeased him? I don't think so, if all you knew was what we find in the first half of this passage.

But that is only half the story. If we look back into the Old Testament we find that these men and women endured all kinds of trouble. They were not spared difficulty. We should certainly see that some of their trials were brought on by their sin, but equally that a good deal of their pain came as a result of the sins of others.

What a different picture we get when we read the rest of the passage in Hebrews! I divided it at the point I did, to bring out the contrast. If you had only the second half of this passage you might suppose that unless you were physically abused to the point of death you could not belong to the Lord at all! See what happens to men and women of faith! Their choices seem to lie between torture, flogging, jail, exile and dying. They could not even be sure that only one of these things would satisfy their persecutors. To be a man of faith means nothing but calamity! Or so it would seem.

Now what can we learn from all of this? It is plain that we cannot read our providences, the events God has decreed for ourselves or others. It requires more wisdom than we have. That does not mean that we should not think about our circumstances when we try to decide what we will do next. We should weigh every fact that touches our lives when we decide what course to take. But no one event, or combination of events, will give us infallible direction. We must pray and then use our judgement in matters where the Word of God does not give specific instructions. We must make our decisions and move on.

There are two kinds of objections that might be raised just here and I want to discuss each of them briefly.

First, someone might look at ancient Israel and say, 'Surely

Israel could tell where it stood with God by whether or not it prospered. That seems to be plain from the Old Testament.' In a general way that would be right, but that does not get us very far for two reasons. To begin with, God dealt with Israel differently from the way he did with any other nation. You can see this by asking yourself this question: 'Did the prosperity of Babylon and Assyria and Persia and Rome prove that God was pleased with them?' Surely not! Their prosperity was God's decretive will — that much is plain. But it proved nothing about their godliness. Then, secondly, this test of prosperity might work for the nation, but it was too general to apply to the individual. We have only to look at the heroes of faith in Hebrews 11 to see that.

A second objection may be a feeling of frustration more than anything else. If we were to put it into words, we might express it like this: 'There are some things that I must know so that I do not make a serious mistake. A marriage partner, for example. Whom should I marry?' Of course, a good deal more could be said along these same lines, and every one of us would understand what the speaker meant. We all have these same types of decisions to make, decisions that will affect the rest of our lives.

But is it in fact certain that we will blunder if we do not know the answers to questions like these? I don't think so. If we are fearful about prayerfully making decisions and acting upon them without a direct word from God, it may be that we have not yet seen how far God influences our lives *when we do not know it*. I am not talking about impressions or feelings or conscious 'leadings'. I mean to say this: even when we are entirely unconscious of his work, God continues to lead us, his people. In Paul's words from Philippians 2:13, 'It is God who works in you to will and to act according to his good purpose.' In the same letter Paul says again, 'He who began a good work in you will carry it on to completion' (Phil. 1:6). These promises extend to all of life. We do not need a perfect understanding of the things that happen to us, and we do not need to look for special impressions or feelings.

Years ago I was talking with a friend named Marie and she began to tell me about a woman she knew, the wife of an internationally known preacher. Calling her friend by name she said, 'She never even walks across the room without first praying about it!' No doubt Marie's friend was a spiritual woman. I have no reason to think otherwise. But it seemed to me then, as it seems to me as I write this, that this woman was under bondage to a mistaken notion. And it was bondage. How could anyone, with the Bible before her, suppose that she would have to get permission from the Lord to cross the room? And how could she live with this idea if she held it seriously?

Of course, Marie may have been exaggerating, but her story stands as an extreme example of a common problem. We do not have enough confidence in the Lord. Part of our liberty in Christ is the freedom he has given us to make decisions. I do not mean to imply that we are free to ignore him when we decide what we will do. Could any Christian suppose such a thing? Surely not! That is why I have said we *prayerfully* exercise our judgement. That means we do so with a sincere desire that the Lord will have his way! And I do mean 'exercise our judgement'! If we tend to be carried away with every transient feeling, we must stop ourselves and talk to ourselves and perhaps write down the pros and cons of the actions we are about to take. All of that is true. But then we must know that the Spirit of the Lord affects our judgement and we can trust him. The Israelite of old had his life fenced in by hundreds of rules. Those rules spoke to dozens of situations daily; they crowded in upon him from dawn to dusk; they gave him guidance in the minutiae of life. But that is not the pattern that God offers his people today. We have only to read the book of Galatians to know that this is the age of relative liberty. 'It is for freedom that Christ has set us free. Stand firm, then, and do not let yourselves be burdened again by a yoke of slavery' (Gal. 5:1).

Let me add a word about impressions, the things that often move Christians to say things like, 'I feel led' to go here or there. No one of us can say whether a given feeling or impression is from the Lord — at least, I cannot — unless it contradicts Scripture. But it seems to me that Christians who think that their impressions are from God often have the vague idea that guidance by impressions was the experience of men and women in the Bible. 'Didn't the Lord speak to Paul and to Peter?' they ask quite reasonably. The answer is: 'Yes, he did.' But that is just the problem with this idea of 'feeling led' to do this or that. When the Lord spoke to Peter and to Paul, they were not called upon to act on impressions. It seems beyond doubt that when the Lord chose to communicate with his people in the Bible he did so plainly, unmistakably. They were not left to 'feel' this or that; he told them what he wanted them to know. That was true whether he used dreams or visions or direct speech. In no way do any of these things justify the widespread use of impressions in our day. The Lord spoke to Paul directly. Now I must face the question, 'Has he spoken to me directly — in so many words?' I cannot say that he has, and I dare not trust my feelings. God has given me his Word and my judgement. Let me use them with godly reverence. Let me distrust myself, but have confidence in him.

At the beginning of this chapter we heard the Lord Jesus rebuke his critics. 'You know how to interpret the appearance of the sky,' he said, 'but you cannot interpret the signs of the times.' Was Christ setting forth a new way to find out God's will? No, he was not. The problem with Jesus' critics was not in their eyes and ears; they were ignorant of the Word of God. They lived in the hour that the prophets had pointed to, in the day that God's Old Testament saints had yearned for. Because they boasted of their superior knowledge the Pharisees and the Sadducees should have been the first to fall down and worship the King. 'You diligently study the Scriptures,' Jesus once said to them. They did indeed study. Jesus spoke the truth. But he had more truth to tell them. 'These are the Scriptures that testify about me,' he added, 'yet you refuse to come to me to have life' (John 5:39-40). He himself was the sign, but they would not see it.

Their problem, like ours, was to submit themselves to the Lord Jesus. The man who does that, and keeps on doing it while he studies God's Word, has found the will of God without infallibly reading God's providence. The man who does not submit to Christ can gaze at events for ever — but he can never find out God's purpose for his life.

'If you believed Moses,' the Lord went on, 'you would believe me, for he wrote about me. But since you do not believe what he wrote, how are you going to believe what I say?' (John 5:46-47). The King stood before them, the choicest sign that God could give them, but they rejected him.

What shall we do? How then shall we live? Our path is plain. God's plan for us is not to be found in his decretive will, in trying to ferret out the meaning behind his sovereign work. God's plan for us is found in his Word, and in the freedom that he sent to us when he sent us the Spirit of his Son, Jesus Christ.

15.
The comfort in God's sovereignty

Some years ago a tornado passed through the Cincinnati area, leaving a good deal of destruction in its wake. Especially hard hit was the suburb of Sayler Park, and in Sayler Park one casualty was a church building struck with such force that the congregation had to meet in the basement the week of the storm.

One local newspaper had the foresight to send out a reporter to hear the pastor's Sunday sermon. The editor no doubt assumed that the preacher would take the disaster as his topic, and that is what he did. He said something like this: 'We have all been upset by the tornado that passed through our area last week. Perhaps we have wondered how God could send such a thing. What I want to do this morning is to remind you that God is a loving God. This was not the work of God. God would not do such a thing. Let's be firm in our faith that God is love.'

It happened that at that time I had a daily radio broadcast in Cincinnati and it was my plan to talk about the tornado on a Monday morning. I was greatly helped, of course, by the reporter's account of his visit to the church, and I was sure that my audience would be interested in the subject. Briefly I said that I could not agree with the pastor's sermon. I understood why he said what he did, and I sympathized with his desire to reassure his people. Then I added: 'If there are forces loose in the world that are not under God's control, that is not good news, but bad news. If, on the other hand, even tornados come from the hands of our Father then they lose their terror. How glad I am that all things are in his power, including tornados!'

My joy in God's sovereignty remains and, indeed, increases as I grow older. But it is also true that to some people God's kingship sounds threatening, as though control by almost anyone would be better than the control of God. I know that they would not put it that way, but what else can I think when I hear men and women who would rarely speak of God's sovereignty go on at great length about the power of Satan in this world? And that is the very thing I hear over and over from Christians around me.

The Bible glories in the sovereignty of God. Look, for example, at Psalm 33:10-11:

'The Lord foils the plans of the nations;
    he thwarts the purposes of the peoples.
But the plans of the Lord stand firm for ever,
    the purposes of his heart through all generations.'

Does the psalmist write reluctantly about God's sovereignty? If he does, you would never guess it from what he goes on to say:

'Blessed is the nation whose God is the Lord,
    the people he chose for his inheritance'
(Ps. 33:12).

The psalmist himself was a part of that nation and one of those elect people. Does he feel any embarrassment at extolling the greatness of God? Is he distraught at God's kingship? To ask these questions is to answer them.

Paul, one of the New Testament writers who has most to say on God's sovereignty, finds no difficulty with this doctrine. He speaks of the God 'who works out everything in conformity with the purpose of his will' (Eph. 1:11). But he calls this same God 'the Father of compassion and the God of all comfort' (2 Cor. 1:3).

Where is the comfort in God's sovereignty? I have already hinted at one part of the answer: the things that take place in this world are under the rule of a wise and loving God.

In the first place, this means that *the Lord knows how to defeat our enemy Satan with Satan's own weapons.* We have already seen how the Lord did that with Paul's thorn in the flesh. The thorn was Satan's weapon, but its effect was to make Paul a more humble and useful servant of Christ.

Here is another instance of the same kind. On 4 June 1739, Charles Wesley wrote in his diary: 'I stood by G[eorge] Whitefield, while he preached on the mount in Blackheath. The cries of the wounded were heard on every side. What has Satan gained by turning him out of the churches?' The devil's weapon was to lock the doors of the churches against Whitefield. Did it work? No, because the Lord intended that his servants preach to hundreds of thousands in the open air. 'The cries of the wounded,' as Wesley called them, were no sure guide to the number of converts, but the gospel was preached to men and women and boys and girls who would never have heard it in a church, and thousands of them proved to be genuinely converted to God. Here was the fulfilment of God's gracious promise: 'No weapon forged against you will prevail' (Isa. 54:17). This was the work of the King.

Here we see another comfort in God's sovereignty: *the hope of revival.* We who belong to Christ long to see great numbers turn to Christ in our own day. What chance is there of that happening? Our hope is in the Lord and in his royal power. If God were not sovereign, it would be up to us to move men's hearts and bring them to Christ. How would we do it? We do not know, we cannot tell, but since the Lord is on the throne we will cry to him. He can unlock hearts as he 'opened [Lydia's] heart to respond to Paul's message' (Acts 16:14).

All Christians agree that the course of history must be in the hands of Christ. What could be sure without his control? In America we look back almost 500 years. Did that time pass without the arm of the Lord guiding the course of events? An anonymous humorist suggests the answer: 'What if Plymouth Rock had landed on the Pilgrims instead of the other way around?' What indeed! The smallest events change the course of nations. As Blaise Pascal wrote in his *Pensées*, 'Had Cleopatra's nose been shorter, the whole history of the world would have been different.' Can we believe in God and not see that he must have guided the path of the ages?

So far in this chapter I have been speaking mainly about God's kingship over large matters, things like the spread of the gospel and the course of history. But the story of the tornado reminds us that God's kingship touches us in our day-by-day lives. I spoke of the tornado as 'coming from the hands of our Father'. There is the personal note, the element of personal comfort. Thinking about the sovereignty of God is meant to do us good daily as we meet with our trials and tests. I want us to look now at various ways that God's sovereignty will comfort us personally.

On the lowest level, it means that *we are not dealing with a frustrated God*! John Piper has asked some questions that show just how important this is: 'Can you imagine what it would be like if the God who ruled the world were not happy? What if God were given to grumbling and pouting and depression like some Jack-and-the-beanstalk giant in the sky? What if God were frustrated and despondent and gloomy and dismal and discontented and dejected? Could we join David and say, "O God, thou art my God, I seek thee; my soul thirsts for thee; my flesh faints for thee, as in a dry and weary land where no water is"'(Psalm 63:1)?' [1]

We know that some ancient Greeks and Romans saw their gods in just this way. The gods envied one another, fought among themselves and generally looked like frustrated human beings who could not find the means to get their own way. 'Spoiled brats!' we might have called them. But our God is content and happy. He is happy with himself, in part because he is King and controls all that he has made.

It is good that God is not frustrated but we can say a great deal more than that. He is not only happy with himself, but he is happy with his people as well, and that means that he treats believers as a father treats his children in a happy home. That is, he loves us and uses his power to do us good.

God's sovereignty does us good all the time, in every circumstance. Earlier, in looking at Romans 8:28, we saw that truth. The point I want to make here is this: that sovereign power of God that always does us good is the power of a father in the highest sense of that word. I know that the name 'father' has so often been abused that some men and women draw back when they hear it. But most of us can imagine what that word might mean if used in the best sense possible, and that is the way Jesus uses it of his Father and ours. The things that do us good do not do so in any random sense. They do us good in the way that a father, in the highest and best sense, does good to his children.

In recent years I have come to love the Lord's Prayer in Matthew 6. I need not quote it here; almost every Christian knows it by heart. One thing that strikes me about it is its context. The Lord Jesus deliberately set it within the framework of God as the Father of his people, so that we may pray with complete confidence that he will do what we ask. In the fifteen verses that begin and end the passage in our English versions (Matt. 6:1-15), Jesus uses the word 'Father' eight times. Others may do good deeds to gain credit in the eyes of men, but as his children we must simply keep our eye on our Father (Matt. 6:1-4). Others may pray from ungodly motives or with low ideas of their gods, but we must think of the one to whom we pray as a Father who has taken responsibility for all the needs of his children (Matt. 6:5-8).

What will our Father do if we pray with confidence in him? He will answer each of the petitions he has taught us to pray! Have you noticed that? Go through the list of things that Jesus taught us to ask for. Which of them will our Father deny us? Not one of them! Every request that we make in the Lord's Prayer is for something that God will do in his own good time, and the things that we ask for ourselves (6:11-13) are what he is doing for us all the time. Daily he gives us bread. Daily he forgives our sins. Daily he delivers us from the power of the Evil One, Satan, so that while we may stumble, we never again will come under the devil's kingship and perish. All this takes great power, dominion and sovereignty on God's part. It is always, for us, however, the sovereignty of our heavenly Father.

I think I hear some reader say, 'Wait a minute! Do you mean to tell me that God's people never go hungry? Is it true that we always get our daily bread, and if that isn't true how do we know that God will do these other things too?' To answer these questions we need to remember one fact: Christians always receive from their Father what they *need*. The Lord's Prayer is very brief. I do not doubt that the request for bread stands for all our daily physical and material needs. It would have been impossible for Jesus to mention all of them; instead he chose the one that seems most pressing and took it to represent them all. But the fact is that there may be some days when we need to go hungry! On those days the Lord will do what he does every other day. As a Father to us, he will give us what we need.

Some people seem to have the idea that a household can get along without discipline, but our Father knows better. An important part of discipline in every home is to deprive us of some of the things that we may want, and may even think we cannot possibly manage without. It may be that being deprived of them will correct one of our grievous faults. But discipline is larger than correction; it is training for life. God has the power to give or to withhold because he is sovereign. He also knows which to choose because he is wise. Both his wisdom and his sovereignty, along with all else that he is, are used for the good of his people. What glorious truth this is! What a privilege to say, 'My Father sent *this*!' whatever it may be.

There is a third way in which the sovereignty of God in his personal dealings with us can be a comfort to us. This is best of all, but it is the hardest to explain and you will need to follow me closely.

The Puritan author Thomas Watson once wrote these words on appreciating God: 'We glorify God, when we are God-admirers; admire his attributes, which are glistering beams by which the divine nature shines forth; his promises which are the charter of free grace, and the spiritual cabinet where the pearl of great price is hid; the noble effects of his power and wisdom in making the world, which is called "the work of his fingers" (Ps. 8:3). To glorify God is to have God-admiring thoughts; to esteem him most excellent, and search for diamonds in this rock only.' I count those words among the most profound I have ever read, and I hope to show in a moment what they have to do with comfort. But for the moment I want to emphasize that this is not, first of all, advice; it is a simple statement of fact. If we want to glorify God we must admire and appreciate him.

Now that seems easy enough. A first step might be to set aside some time to think about God. We cannot think admiring thoughts of God if we are not thinking of him at all. But this will not get us very far for two reasons, one obvious and the other not so obvious. The obvious reason is this: we may set aside time to think about God, but as surely as we do so we will have a fight to keep our minds on God. And when our minds are on the fight they are not on God!

But here is the really important problem: we cannot admire anyone, just by planning to do so. It may be a great thing to admire God, but you cannot grit your teeth and say, 'I'm going to admire God!' and that is that. There has to be something in God that calls forth your admiration. That is the heart of the matter. Of course everything about God is admirable. I would not want to deny that — in fact, I want to affirm it with all my being. But we are, in part at least, products of the culture around us, and there is such a thing as our Christian culture, the influence of those whom we see preaching on television or hear on the radio, and there is the effect of other Christians who are our friends and the leaders of our churches. No one, I suppose, would care to deny that this culture exists or that it influences us. The thing that worries me about it, however, does not seem to be noticed by some others: God as he is seen in the Scriptures often seems to be neglected in this culture. Man seems so important — what he does and says, what he feels and thinks. Satan so often seems so powerful that God is made to seem helpless. Satan seems to go on his merry way, doing as he pleases, but God's hands seem to be tied, unless Christians co-operate with him. At least that is the message I think I hear.

Suppose that I am right; suppose that Christians do not have high thoughts about God — what can I do? To begin with, I must remember that I cannot read the minds and hearts of my fellow believers. Their thoughts may be higher than I know. In fact, no doubt they are, since every true Christian must be a worshipper of God and no one can worship God without seeing something of his glory. Every Christian is an admirer of God or he would not be a Christian.

But my experience was this: understanding the sovereignty of God led me to much larger views of God. Surely I admired God before; I do not want to minimize that. But when I came to see that God rules in this world in a way that I did not formerly dream of, it came like a meteor flash into my life. There was a glory about God that I had not seen before! What a revelation it was — and is! And what a comfort! How easy my heart could be, how much peace I could have if I served a God like this God! That was my feeling then, and that is my feeling now as I sit here and write about it. My greatest frustration is my inability to convey this to others! May the Lord enable me to do so.

I still have no solution for wandering thoughts. Suppose I set aside time to think of God and nothing else, can I do it? No, I cannot. It is like the offer of a ten-million dollar prize for standing in the corner for half an hour and thinking of nothing but a white deer! Twenty-nine of those minutes would be spent in thinking of the prize!

On the other hand, minds can wander in more than one direction. A man who admires God may not always be able to keep his mind on his work. He may be surprised at his workbench by thoughts of God. He may cry out, 'We have a God!' in the midst of either pleasure or pain. He may be moved to tears of joy and wonder and astonishment at the splendid works and endowments of his Creator and Redeemer. There is comfort in the greatness of God. You may rise above yourself and your interests and find delight in God, and in that very process you will comfort your own heart in a way that nothing else in the world can match. Yes, your mind may wander in that way as well!

Finally, let me ask and answer the question, is there anything you can do to come to admire God further? Yes, there is. You can read the Bible with the admiration of God in mind. That is first; that is basic. Throughout this book I have sought to take my readers by the hand and teach you Scripture. I am not ashamed of that task. As a teacher it belongs to me, it is my calling. I must do it and I want to do it. You must carry on without me, however. Other teachers will help you, no doubt; that is all to the good. We all need teachers; we must all be taught. But when all is said, you must read God's Word with this in mind: what do I learn here about God himself? I do not deny that we may read God's Word to answer other questions, such things as 'How can I get on with my neighbours?' and 'How can I have a godly family?' Those are important questions and the Bible gives us the essential answers to them. But the Bible is a book about God, and you will live in poverty of mind and heart unless you use it for the first purpose for which God gave it, to come to know him and to grow in knowing him.

I hope you will look for his sovereignty as you read. If you do, you will find the personal comforts I have been telling you about. On the lowest level you will find an unfrustrated God; that is no small thing! Next you will find a Father, one who cares for all your needs, whether you recognize them or not. Finally you will begin to feel as never before the wonder of our God. I pray that you will not escape a genuine taste of his glory. Take a deep drink! Once you savour his majesty you will be happily trapped as an admirer of God for ever.

Note

1. John Piper develops this idea in the book, *Desiring God,* Multnomah Press, 1986, p. 24f. The entire book is well worth reading to raise our consciousness of the greatness and glory of God.

Appendix I
Saved Israelites and the church

It is not easy to see exactly how Israel relates to the church. That fact has caused a good deal of division among God's people. This appendix explains my own understanding of this relationship.

Readers may be familiar with one of two views:

1. Some say there is little difference between the church and Israel. The people of God in the Old Testament are called Israel and in the New Testament they are called the church, but organically they are one people throughout history. Distinctions that may be drawn between them are minor.

2. Some say that Israel and the church are utterly distinct entities, each with its own future. The sharpest distinction must be drawn between them or confusion results.

Both of these views can muster a good deal of plausible support from Scripture, but neither of them, it seems to me, reflects all that the Bible teaches on the subject. It is clear from the New Testament that there is a certain continuity between Old and New Testament saints which the second view ignores. On the other hand, the New Testament has a great deal to say about discontinuity when it emphasizes the new humanity formed in Christ. It is impossible to treat these differences as incidental.

The solution to this difficulty is suggested by the nineteenth-century theologian, J. L. Dagg: 'In the words of Christ…, the church is represented as a building. The beginning of an edifice may be dated back to the first movement in preparing the materials. In this view the church was begun, when Abel, Enoch, Noah, and Abraham first exercised faith. But in another view, the building was commenced when the materials were brought together in their proper relation to Jesus Christ. To the Old Testament saints, until gathered under Christ with the saints of the present dispensation, Paul attributes a sort of incompleteness, which may be not unaptly compared to the condition of building materials not yet put together: "These all, having obtained a good report through faith, received not the promise: God having provided some better thing for us, that they without us should not be made perfect."' [1]

Let's see how Dagg's statement compares with what the Bible teaches about the people of God.

First we must see that no one can ever be saved outside of Christ. 'Salvation is found in no one else, for there is no other name under heaven given to men by which we must be saved' (Acts 4:12). Christians agree on this.

But to be *in* Christ is to be part of his body, that is, the church. This seems clear from Ephesians 1:20-23: '[God] raised him from the dead and seated him at his right hand in the heavenly realms, far above all rule and authority, power and dominion, and every title that can be given, not only in the present age but also in the one to come. And God placed all things under his feet and appointed him to be head over everything for the church, which is his body...' Here we see that all the enormous power and authority of Christ is exercised 'for the church'. If there were any other body of redeemed people in the universe, they would be included in the 'all things under his feet', and they would be under Christ *for the benefit of the church*. Those (like dispensationalists), however, who distinguish saved Israel from the church never argue that such Israelites existed for the church's benefit.

This passage throws light on a later one, where Paul says that 'Christ loved the church and gave himself up for her' (Eph. 5:25). The simplest way to understand Paul here is to suppose he has all the redeemed of every age in view. The verses from chapter 1 confirm that view. Again, to be in Christ would be to be in the church, the group for whom he died.

On the other hand, Christ's church does not appear to have been formed until the present age. As Dagg said, 'The church is represented as a building', and 'The building was commenced when the materials were brought together in their proper relation to Jesus Christ.' The new nation, or the new humanity, considered as a unit, was not formed in Old Testament times. It awaited the coming of

Christ. When 'Abel, Enoch, Noah, and Abraham first exercised faith' they became stones that would be included in the church. But the formation of Christ's church, his body, did not take place until the new age.

As Martyn Lloyd-Jones has written on Ephesians 2:15: '*The Church is something absolutely new* that has been brought into being, something that was not there before... The Church is not a sort of coalition of Jews and Gentiles; something absolutely new has come into being which was just not there before. Creation! — "for to create in himself of twain one new man" ... Indeed we can call it *a new humanity*. And that, it seems to me, is the best way of looking at it. In Jesus Christ, and as a result of His perfect work, something entirely new has come into being. What is it? It is a new humanity.'[2]

Again Lloyd-Jones shows that this body came into being in New Testament times: 'The old has been done away with. The Lord Jesus Christ Himself put it like this once and for ever in a most important statement from this standpoint, Matthew 21 verse 43. Addressing the Jews he said, "Therefore I say unto you, the kingdom of God shall be taken from you and given to a nation bringing forth the fruits thereof." That new nation is the Church. The Jews as such have ceased to be the special people of God. There is a new nation.'[3] The church is a *new* nation.

Compare Ephesians 2:20-21 with what Lloyd-Jones says here. Christians are said to be 'built on the foundation of the apostles and prophets, with Christ Jesus himself as the chief cornerstone. In him the whole building is joined together and rises to become a holy temple in the Lord.'

In Old Testament times there had been a temple where God met his people. But a day came when the Lord left that temple for ever. His plan was to inhabit a new temple. That temple is Christ's body, the church. It did not exist as a building or temple before Christ came to form it by his cross. It is built on the apostles and New Testament prophets.[4]

In conclusion, then, I agree with Dagg. All of God's elect who have already been saved are now part of the new humanity, the church. But the church did not exist in Old Testament times as a unit under the headship of the Lord Jesus Christ. The same Holy Spirit who formed the Head, the Lord Jesus, in the womb of Mary also formed and is forming his body. By understanding the Scriptures in

this way we can see both the continuity and discontinuity that exists
between Israel and the church.

Notes

1. J. L. Dagg, *Manual of Theology*, Gano Books, 1982, Second Part, pp. 138-9. The
biblical quotation is from Hebrews 11:39-40 which Dagg attributes to the apostle
Paul.
2. D. Martyn Lloyd-Jones, *God's Way of Reconciliation*, Baker Book House, 1972,
pp. 214-216. All italics in these quotations are his.
3. *Ibid.*, p. 218
4. 'The position that the term prophets as here used refers to the Old Testament
bearers of that appellative, such as Moses, Elijah, Isaiah, Jeremiah, etc... is open
to serious objections...' These words of Hendriksen are followed by his reasons for
confining the prophets here to New Testament prophets. William Hendriksen,
Exposition Of Ephesians, Baker Book House, 1967, p. 142.

Appendix II
Judgement and our inheritance in the new earth

The German scholar Theodor Zahn (1838-1933) has shown the basic connection between judgement and our receipt of the blessings God has promised us in an exposition of the sealed book ('scroll' — NIV) found in Revelation chapters 5-6. This was brought to my attention by G. R. Beasley-Murray's Commentary on the book of Revelation in the *New Century Bible Commentary Series*, p. 121. Since Zahn's discussion will not be available to most readers, I want to quote it at length. The following is verbatim, except that I have taken the liberty to translate a few Greek and Latin words into English and I have broken the passage, which is a single paragraph in the original, into several paragraphs for ease in reading it.

'The word *scroll* itself permits of a great many interpretations, but for the readers of that time it was designated by the seven seals on its back beyond the possibility of mistake. Just as in Germany before the introduction of money orders, everyone knew that a letter sealed with five seals contained money, so the most simple member of the Asiatic churches knew that a scroll made fast with seven seals was a *testament*...

'When the testator dies the testament is brought forward, and, when possible, opened in the presence of the seven witnesses who sealed it; i.e. unsealed, read aloud, and executed. The making of a will assumes that the death of the testator lies in the future, while its opening and execution imply that his death has taken place.

'But, as is well known, the Christians of earliest times, although mindful of the fact that God does not die (Heb. 9: 16f.) and that all comparisons are lame in some respects, do not hesitate to imagine the property supposed to belong to God, to his Son, and to his church, and the entrance of the church into possession of it, under the figure of inheritance (heritage and inheriting), and accordingly, to compare the assurance of these properties on God's part with a testamentary disposition. Jesus himself uses the figure (Luke 22:29; cf. Matt. 5:5; 21:38; 25:34; Mark 12:7; Luke 20:14), and all the New Testament writers (Gal. 3:15 - 4:7; Rom. 8:17ff.; Eph. 1:14,18; 5:5; Col. 1:12; 3:24; 1 Peter 1:4; Heb. 1:2; 6:17; 8: 6; 9:15ff.; James 2:5).

'So also here, the document fastened with seven seals is an easily understood symbol of the promise and assurance by God to his church of the future kingdom. This irrevocable disposition of God, similar to a man's testamentary disposition of his goods, has long ago occurred, been documented and sealed, but not yet carried out. The inheritance is still laid up in heaven (1 Peter 1:4), and the testament therefore not yet opened and executed. That its content has been proclaimed through the prophets, and through Jesus and the Spirit which rules in the church (1 Cor. 2:10), and has to a certain extent become known, does not destroy its resemblance to a sealed testament waiting to be opened, any more than the oral communication of a human testator, concerning the content of his will, destroys the importance of the document and renders its opening unnecessary. Apart from the fact that the heritages promised to the church are to exceed all previous human experience, imagination, and anticipation (1 Cor. 2:7-9; 13:12; 1 John 3:2), and that not until they are delivered over will their true nature be disclosed (Rom. 8:18), the point of comparison, since the promise of future glory and royal dominion is likened to a sealed will, lies not so much in the fact that no one *knows* the contents, as that they still *await realization.*

'No one is authorized to open the testament and thereby to put into execution the will of God therein laid down, except the Lamb, who by dying gained the victory like a lion, and delivered the church (5:5,9f.). The returning Christ will open the testament of God and execute it...

'[The breaking of the seals] is well adapted to show what, through the returned Christ, *preparatory to it* must precede the final fulfilment of the promise. The visions which occur as the first six seals are opened naturally bear upon the contents of the still unopened testament in this way:

1. The Word of God must take its victorious way through the world (6:2; cf. Matt.24:14);

2. Bloody wars must come (v. 3f.; cf. Matt. 24:6; Mark 13:7);

3. Times of scarcity (v. 5f.);

4. Plagues destroying part of the people (v. 7f.; cf. Matt. 24:7; Luke 21:11); then

5. Bloody persecutions of the church, the punishment for which is delayed (vv. 9-11; cf. Matt. 24: 9; Mark 13:11-13); but at last

6. Events in nature which are to convulse the world and fill earthly despots with terrible anticipation of the wrath of God and of the Lamb which is about to be outpoured upon them (vv. 12-17; cf. Matt. 24:29f.; Luke 21:25; 23:30).'[1]

We need not agree with Zahn's every detail. Identifying the first seal has been difficult for scholars and many think that it must symbolize judgement, as the other five clearly do. But Zahn's explanation of the sealed scroll joins judgement and our inheritance closely together in a way in keeping with all the New Testament. When Christ sets out to give us our heritage he finds it wrapped up with judgement upon the earth. Opening the seals brings various judgements. When they have all been opened, the will is executed and God's people have their inheritance, including the new earth.

Reference

1. Theodor Zahn, *Introduction To The New Testament,* T & T Clark, 1909, vol. III, pp. 393-6.

Index of names and subjects

Scripture index